THE DYNAMICS OF CRITICISM IN
T.S. ELIOT

THE DYNAMICS OF CRITICISM IN
T.S. ELIOT

MOHAMMAD HANIEF

ATLANTIC PUBLISHERS AND DISTRIBUTORS

Published by
ATLANTIC PUBLISHERS AND DISTRIBUTORS
B-2, Vishal Enclave, Opp. Rajouri Garden, New Delhi-27
Phones : 5413460, 5429987
e-mail : info@atlantibooks.com

Sales Office
4215/1, Ansari Road, Darya Ganj, New Delhi-110 002
Phones : 3273880, 3285873, 3280451
Fax : 91-11-3285873
web site : www.atlanticbooks.com

ISBN 81-7156-926-9

Typeset at
APD Computer Graphics, Delhi

Printed in India at
Nice Printing Press, Delhi

Dedicated to
AMNA

PREFACE

Books on Eliot are usually about Eliot's poetry; here, I have made a systematic and detailed study of his critical essays and prose-writings. Some parts of the book (for example, Eliot's criticisms of novels and novelists) are so new that I take them tantamount to discovery. I have referred to Xerox copies of uncollected articles and reviews of Eliot, and one would be surprised to know how many of Eliot's writings still remain uncollected.

The present book aims at exposing many prevalent half-truths, facetious and fallacious generalisations about Eliot. For example, Eliot's definition of poetry as an "escape from personality" is notoriously known and widely circulated, but the fact that Eliot sincerely and seriously insisted on the value and significance of personality in works of art in many of his essays is hardly believed by his readers.

I express my indebtedness to Professor Leonard Unger who has encouraged me a great deal.

MOHAMMAD HANIEF

CONTENTS

CONTENTS

1
Introduction

The subject of my thesis is *The Theory and Practice of Criticism in T.S. Eliot*. My concern is mainly with Eliot's prose work rather than his poetry. Professor Grand T. Webster in an article[1] has said that it is time to look at Eliot's critical writings without their poetic halo — and that they have merits unconnected with Eliot's poetry. The subject in comprehensive, and I have tried as far as posssible, to narrow the focus in order to direct it with force and sharpness at a particular frontier.

The books written about Eliot are chiefly concerned with his poetry and plays and only partially with his literary criticism. My attempt has been to make a systematic study of Eliot's criticism. Apart from the published books of Eliot, I have utilised materials usually inaccessible, in the form of reviews, introductions and prefaces, lying in different journals and periodicals of the past like *The Egoist, The Times Literary Supplement, The Dial, The Athenaeum* and *The Hudson Review*. It is my attempt to assess his contribution by considering his theorisings on general topics and individual authors and to find out the permanent and the reactionary, the real and the sham, the temporarily useful and the consistently illuminating in him.

I have included specially a chapter on Eliot's criticism of the novel and novelists because during the course of my research I discovered that Eliot had reviewed many novelists. He has written on Henry James, Mark Twain, Beyle and Balzac, James Joyce, Turgenev, besides an obituary on Virginia Woolf. And I have added a short study of Eliot's prose style and critical method.

Though Eliot's formulations are taken to be the byproduct of

Eliot's poetry-workshop, it is possible that Eliot the critic may survive Eliot the poet. Eliot's poetry appears to us, sometimes, as a technical triumph. In the realm of poetry, one feels, one cannot go too far in Eliot's direction, as Eliot's poetry is found at times wanting in the human substratum.

T.S. Eliot was born in 1888 at St. Louis, Missouri. He belonged to a cultivated New England family. In 1908 be entered Harvard University. There he attended the lectures of George Santayana and Irving Babbitt, and was influenced by them. In 1910-11, he was in Paris, studying French literature and Philosophy at the Sorbonne. Returning to America, he continued his study of Philosophy at Harvard and also received some instruction in Sanskrit and Indian Philosophy, spending a year in the mazes of Patanjali's metaphysics. He visited Germany on a travelling scholarship in 1913 and, in the first year of the war, was studying philosophy at Merton College, Oxford. He settled in England and his first mature poems were published in English periodicals in 1915-16. He taught for a time at Highgate School and later worked in a London bank. After the war, he was an active contributor to London literary periodicals. He founded and edited *The Criterion*. He also became a director of the publishing firm, Faber and Faber. He was naturalised as a British subject in 1927 and, in a volume of essays published in 1928, described his general point of view as "Classicist in literature, Royalist in politics and Anglo-Catholic in religion."

Eliot gives a hint about the background of his essays, specially his early critical essays. He writes in *To Criticise the Critic* :

> I was in reaction not only against Georgian poetry, but against Georgian criticisim; I was writing in a context which the reader of to-day has either forgotten, or has never experienced.[2]

In the eighteen-eighties, "Art for Art's sake" was in vogue. It was a return to the Romantic pleasure-principle in literature. And criticism was taken to be, "the adventure of a soul among masterpieces."[3] The critic was supposed just to talk about himself with reference to an author. Eliot said in his essay on Dryden : "The twentieth century is still the nineteenth, although it may in time acquire its own character."⁴ Shaw was one of the earliest writers of the new century to make "interrogation" an article of his faith. "For Art's sake alone," said Shaw, "I would not face the toil of writing a single sentence."⁵

Eliot at his best, like Aristotle, substituted scientific inquiry, dispassionate dissection and assessment for subjectivism and the vagueness of impressionism. Nor does he favour the sociological or the psychological criticism :

> The Psychological and the Sociological are probably the two best advertised varieties of modern criticism; but the number of ways in which the problems of criticism are approached was never before so great or so confusing....Criticism seems to have separated into several diverse kinds.⁶

Comparison and analysis, as Eliot says, are the chief tools of criticism. According to Eliot, a critic should have a highly developed sense of fact and a critic's task is to make the reader possessed of facts. In matters of great importance, Eliot points out, the critic should not make judgments of worse and better; he must simply elucidate.

T.S. Eliot is a very great critic indeed. He is, after all, a critic of comprehensive taste. He does not hesitate or feel shy in modifying or revising his critical opinions and attitudes. When the light of a new experience is cast upon him, he shows his readiness to look at a work of art from a different angle. In his essay "The Metaphysical Poets" (1921), Eliot extends much praise to John Donne's poetry for its speech rhythms, elaboration of a figure of speech to the furthest stage, and the telescoping of images and multiplied associations.

After 10 years, i.e., in 1931, Eliot is somewhat critical of Donne's poetry and the fashion for it. A Garland for John Donne, Eliot writes that it is vain to deny that there is an element of fashion in our enjoyment and exploitation of Donne. He wishes simply to distinguish between the absolute and the relative in popularity and to recognise in the relative (both when a poet is unduly preferred and when be is unduly ignored) an element of the reasonable, the just and the significant. He acknowledges that Donne is a greater master of language than Crashaw, Herbert, and Vaughan, but deplores the lack of a consistent viewpoint or some philosophic attitude to life in his work. In 1931, he says that Donne's mind should have been "philosophical" instead of being "legal and controversial." He writes further in the same essay, A *Garland for John Donne,* that Donpe is more interested in "ideas" themselves as objects than in the truth of the ideas. Donne's scoffing attitude towards the fickleness of woman may be hardly more than immature bravado.

Being impressed and guided by Ezra Pound, Eliot at one stage attached importance only to the criticism of critics who are themselves poets and practitioners. Later on, Eliot god rid of this bias and modified his views.

Between 1,933 and 1946, Eliot revised and reversed most of his evaluations. And this feature in him is not to be condemned; it is rather to be appreciated as it points to his developing and progressing experience. Tennyson, whom Eliot scorned in 1922, was the object of serious and elevated commendation in 1936. In the same way, Yeats who, in 1922, was said to be outside the English tradition, was praised in the highest terms in 1933.

By 1934, Eliot had fruitfully contradicted or modified many of his literary and critical judgments implied in the essay "The Metaphysical Poets." He had praised not only Tennyson and Yeats but also Wordsworth and Coleridge who were more more or less rejected in 1921. In 1937, when questioned[7] during a radio interview on the B.B.C. about what he regarded as great poetry, he replied that Wordsworth's "Resolution and Independence" and Coleridge's "Ode on Dejection" were probably the "touchstones of greatness". This is, of course, very different from what Eliot had said earlier. In 1936, Eliot quite condemned Milton, and charged him for corrupting the English language. Eliot had formed the impression that Milton could only be an unwholesome influence for any writer of any generation. In 1947, Eliot is not wholly of the same view :

> I repeat : the remoteness of Milton's verse from ordinary speech, his invention of his own poetic language, seems to me one of the marks of his greatness.[8]

And Eliot points out the cause :

> We cannot, in literature, any more than in the rest of life, live in 'a perpetual state of revolution. If every generation of poets made it their task to bring poetic diction up-in-date with the spoken language, poetry would fail in one of its most important obligations. For poetry should help ... refine the language of the time, but prevent it from changing too rapidly; a development of language at too great a speed would be a development in the sense of a progressive deterioration, and that is our danger to-day.[9]

In "Tradition and the Individual Talent", Eliot defines poetry in terms of impersonality, as "escape from emotion" and "escape from personality." In his essay on W.B. Yeats, he is of the opinion that the great impersonality is forged of personality, that is, when there has been much of intensely felt emotional experience on the part of the poet.

In "The Function of Criticism" Eliot stresses the fact-finding duty of a critic and opines that a future critic may put even the laundry bills of Shakespeare to some use. Eliot is in favour of storing a piece of fact, even of the lowest degree. But in "The Frontiers of Criticism," he is very critical of the source-hunting and genesis-seeking aspect of a critic. He advises the critic to go directly to a work of art and analyse it and appreciate it, instead of indulging in extraneous details. That Wordsworth secretly loved Dorothy Wordsworth may be true, but it does not, as Eliot says, add to our enjoyment and understanding of the Lucy poems. Eliot is critical of "the explanation of poetry by examination of its sources."

> For myself, I can only say that a knowledge of the springs which released a poem is not necessarily a help towards understanding the poem : too much information about the origins of the poem may even break my contact with it...."[10]

Thus, we see that Eliot's critical mind has solidity, comprehensiveness, awareness and range. His critical sensibility is always developing and widening its frontiers and gaining richness and complexity. In "Shakespeare and the Stoicism of

Seneca" (1927), Eliot writes that the poet makes poetry, the metaphysiciam makes metaphysics, the bee makes honey, the spider secretes a filament; one can hardly say that any of these agents believes; he merely does. In "Goethe as the Sage" (1955), Eliot writes :

> ...I have written...in the past...that the poet need not believe a philosophical idea he has chosen to embody in his verse. Professor Heller is, no doubt, quite right in contradicting me. For such a suggestion would appear to be a justification of insincerity, and would annihilate all poetic values except those of technical accomplishment.[11]

And Eliot says further in the same essay that wisdom and poetry are inseparable in poets of the highest rank. Hence, to Eliot, finally, poetry or literature in general without tough reasonableness, consistent viewpoint, some system of thought or plausible belief, is like coffee without caffeine or tea without tannin.

In his numerous essays and lectures, he dwells upon almost every important aspect of literature and criticism.

He says[12] brilliantly that the discipline of the critic is to learn on what grounds "not" to admire the poets whom he primarily loves, and to learn to love a little those poets whom he only frigidly admires. He points[13] out that one of the tests — though it may be only a negative test — of anything really new and genuine, seems to be its capacity for exciting aversion among — "lovers of poetry." In addition to the literary problems, he is seriously concerned with the major issues which vex the minds of modern thinkers. He is concerned with the survival of culture and civilisation with the problem of values, and with religion and its impact on the creative mind. Thus, as a critic of life and letters, Eliot surveys the whole panorama of human experience. As a literary critic, Eliot is of opinion — that the literariness of a work of art can be ascertained by literary standards, but as a critic of life he maintains that the greatness of literature cannot be ascertained by purely literary considerations. Such statements of Eliot only confirm the richness and complexity of his critical ideas and formulations.

Professor Wilbur Scott, in his book *Five Approaches of Literary Criticism,* writes about the five categories of modern criticism — Moral, Psychological, Sociological, Formalistic and Archetypal — and rightly says that a critic deserving of continued attention, will not stay within the confines of a single approach; on the contrary, he will employ any method or methods in combination — which best suit his knowledge, his particular critical sensitiveness and the work of art before him. Such is the case with Eliot. As a critic, Eliot, at his best, can hardly be said to represent only one category of criticism. Professor Wilbur Scott, in his book, lists Eliot in the category of moral criticism by including the essay — "Religion and Literature". In fact, even in his later stage, Eliot as critic does not take the role of a preacher or a theologian. He wants to assert that literature is not merely a chimera of sensation. He makes a pertinent statement in 1956, that a critic who is interested in nothing but "literature would have very little to say to us, for his literature would be a pure abstraction." And Eliot has not "little" but "much" to say to us because he has other interests and beliefs as well. The primary interest of a critic in writing criticism, Eliot points out, is to help his readers to understand and enjoy. But he must have other interests; for the literary critic is not merely a technical expert who has learned the rules to be observed by the writers he criticises. The critic, Eliot continues, must be the whole man, a man with convictions and principles, with knowledge and experience of life. Eliot's statement about the primacy of the supernatural over the natural life[14] would appeal to any serious person who, in moments of inattention to mundane affairs, thinks over the immensity, the complexity, the mystery and the purpose behind the Universe. It is quite natural on the part of man to attempt to understand, like a metaphysician, the vast panorama of events, unaccountable sufferings and agonies of human life, and the meaning behind the creation of the world. Some kind of belief or some system of thought regarding human life and the universe is thus gradually forced upon any thinking and feeling man. And the critic in Eliot is the whole man, a man with knowledge and experience of life. Eliot as critic cannot be defined by being called a literary critic in the limited sense of theological or moral or formalistic. Eliot does not bargain literature for theology. He praises, Tennyson's *In Memoriam* highly, for it represents in Eliot's words the concern for "the loss of man" rather than "the gain of God."[15]

Eliot uses the word "moral" in the wider and profounder sense at several places. In a review, "Beyle and Balzac",[16] he says that the superiority of Henri Beyle and Dostoevsky over Balzac is a moral one, in the sense that Beyle's work achieves greater reality and greater exploration and analysis of it. The aura of Balzac, Eliot says very aptly, sputters and goes out. In Balzac, Eliot continues, the fantastic element is not an extension of reality but an atmosphere thrown upon reality.

Eliot's opinions regarding literature and criticism are useful, illuminating and varied. He has focused light on varied aspects of many literary problems. Eliot writes in *The use of Poetry*[17] that it is reasonable to be on guard against views which claim too much for poetry, as well as to protest against those which claim too little, to recognise a number of uses for poetry, without admitting that poetry must, always and everywhere, be subservient to any of them. In the essay, "The Perfect Critic", he is against the dogmatic and the purely "technical" critic for he takes criticism to be the "disinterested exercise of intelligence."

In a review entitled "The Problem of the Shakespeare Sonnets"[18], Eliot says that there are two points on which the literary critic ought to support the textual critic : in his reticence about the "autobiographical" element and in his reliance upon exact stylistic texts rather than upon enthusiasm. And he adds, that when a literary critic attempts the ascription of a poem to an author, on the basis of his "feeling", he will go very wrong indeed. In his essay — "Goethe as the Sage", he writes aptly that literary criticism is an activity which must constantly define its own boundaries, also it must constantly be going beyond them, for he believes that one cannot go very far with Dante, or Goethe, without touching upon theology and philosophy, and ethics and politics.

F.R. Leavis, in a review "Eliot's Stature as Critic" brings serious charges against Eliot as critic. He writes : "What was not at once apparent to all of those impressed was that some of the ideas, attitudes and valuations put into currency by Eliot were arbitrary...."[19] And more : "It is not then a coherent conception of art that is figured in Eliot's artist'. 'The more perfect the artist, the more completely separate in him will be the man who suffers and the mind which creates'....No one with Tolstoy in mind as the type of the great creative writer could have advanced the proposition : 'separate', for such a use, is not a possible word, whether one thinks of Tolstoy or Lawrence....or Shakespeare or George Eliot or Mark Twain....It clearly is a most significant defeat of intelligence that presents itself to us in Eliot's essay.[20]

Here, it seems, Dr. Leavis has not taken the context and the background of Eliot's essay and expression into consideration. Even apart from the context and time, Eliot's critical notion is not really inappropriate. Good art is only possible when the artist is not overswayed by his suffering or excessive emotional experience.

Some may not place Lawrence and Tolstoy in one category as Dr. Leavis has done. Lawrence, though a supreme artist, "whom it is idle to criticise", seems to miss the greatness of Tolstoy. Tolstoy, it may be agreed, is in the profounder sense more "moral" than Lawrence. Regarding Lawrence, one is rightly reminded of Eliot's words — "the tragic waste of power."

F.R. Leavis uses harsh words like "the absurdity of the dictum"[21] concerning Eliot's important formulation about the perfect artist. One is inclined to disagree with Dr. Leavis when he finds in the definition a significant defect of intelligence. In the early part of the twentieth century Eliot had to play the part of an iconoclast. He was obliged to exaggerate his stand in order to demolish the lingering romantic facades and habits. Eliot like Arnold is a master of phrases and definitions. F.R. Leavis presents more damaging points about Eliot : "Eliot as critic has in general been not a profoundly or wholly engaged one....There is a sense in which he is too much of an intellectual."[22]

My claim for considering Eliot as a major critic rests on the fact that he is essentially a developing personality with sufficient courage and conviction to change or modify his views. In his early phase as a critic he stressed certain values which urgently required stressing. Naturally, Eliot emphasised the artefact, technical excellence in verse, structure and precision of expression as against the nineteenth century attitude. Later, Eliot's interests widened as well as deepened and in fidelity to experience he modified his views. This is not intellectual flirtation with ideas; it is fidelity to the truth of one's vision. Unfortunately, Dr. Leavis has written about Eliot in a pejorative and depreciative vein, that he is "too much of an intellectual."

We do not have this kind of impression about Eliot, the critic, as a whole. He is not insensitive to the emotional value and aspect of literature. While introducing the poems of Miss Marianne Moore, he takes note of their emotional value :

> To the moderately intellectual, the poems may appear to be intellectual exercises; only to those whose intellection moves more easily will they immediately appear to have emotional value.[23]

And later :

> We have to choose whatever subject-matter allows us the most powerful and most secret release; and that is a personal affair.[24]

While introducing the poetry of Harold Monro, Eliot extends much praise to its originality and the personal vision. Eliot says :

> ...It was not indeed until re-reading the whole of his published work, I recognised completely, how distinctly, in his whole work, the vision is the personal vision of Harold Monro.[25]

Eliot marks very appreciatively the note of individuality in the poetry of Harold Monro and says that Monro does not express the spirit of an age; he expresses the spirit of one man, but that so faithfully, that his poetry will remain as one variety of the infinite number of possible expressions of the tortured human consciousness. Eliot is not a "classicist" or "intellectual" in the limiting sense. At times he strikes us, in a very good sense, as having the sensibility of a fine romanticist. Eliot writes :

> Why, for all of us, out of all that we have heard, seen, felt, in a lifetime, do certain images recur, charged with emotion, rather than others. The song of one bird, the

> leap of one fish, at a particular place and time, the
> scent of one flower, an old woman on a German
> mountain-path....such memories may have symbolic
> value, but of what we cannot tell, for they come to
> represent the depths of feeling into which we cannot
> peer.[26]

Eliot is not unfeeling to "the depths of feeling into which
we cannot peer." He whole-heartedly approves[27] and gives full
assent to A.E. Housman's explanation of poetry : "....If I were
obliged not to define poetry, but to name the class of things to
which it belongs, I should call it a secretion; whether a natural
secretion, like the pearl in the oyster...."

Eliot at one place writes that the desire to read the poetry of
Pope is a test of one's love for poetry. This may sound somewhat
exaggerated but it is antidotal to one's confinement to only one
kind of poetry and of only one age. He exalts, Dryden's poetry
but, at the same time, he is not ignorant of its limitations. This
kind of attitude on the part of Eliot is to be understood in his
own words. He writes in this context while introducing a book
of Leone Vivante :

> He [the critic or artist-aesthetician] should not be
> ashamed of exalting neglected artists of the past or of
> other languages and civilisations, even above their merit,
> in order to call attention to their value; if he is
> convinced that these are the most profitable subjects of
> study, and the best possible influences upon his own
> contemporaries and juniors.[28]

Eliot has a singular style of his own in the sense that he has
no style; still it has unique force, clarity and flow. His style is
lucid or translucent though the ideas and experiences may be
complex.

One of the most captivating qualities of Eliot's prose writings
is that they are always *interesting*, besides being minutely critical.
This quality does not leave Eliot even when he is expressing his
most serious views about literature and criticism. No other critic
except Dr. Johnson has this.

Delmore Schwartz has written an article with the title — "The
Literary Dictatorship of T.S. Eliot".[29] To talk of the dictatorship

of Eliot both as critic and poet, is not altogether unjustified. It is true in the sense that the best criticism of our time is usually Eliot-oriented. The New Criticism has virtually taken its start from Eliot and I.A. Richards, although Eliot is disarmingly modest about it :

> I have been somewhat bewildered to find, from time to time, that I am regarded as one of the ancestors of modern criticism, if too old to be a modern critic myself ....though I hope that as an editor I gave the new criticism, or some of it, encouragement and an exercise ground in *The Criterion*.[30]

REFERENCES

1. "Eliot as critic : the man behind the mask", *Criticism* (Published by Wayne State University Press), 1966, Vol. VIII, No. 4, p. 336.

2. To *Criticize the Critic*, p. 16 (Faber & Faber 1965).

3. Anatole France, Preface to *On Life and Letters* (First Series).

4. *Selected Essays*, p. 305 (Faber & Faber).

5. Epistle Dedicatory to *Man and Superman*.

6. Introduction to *The Use of Poetry and the Use of Criticism*, p. 27 (Faber & Faber 1932).

7. *Literary Opinion in America*, edited by M.D. Zabel, p. 573.

8. *Selected Prose*, p. 142 (Faber & Faber 1953; Penguin).

9. *Ibid.*, p. 148.

10. *On Poetry and Poets*, p. 112 (2nd Impression, University Press, Glasgow).

11. *Ibid.*, pp. 222-23.

12. "Donne in our Time", an essay by T.S. Eliot, pub. by Peter Smith, 1958.

13. *Selected Poems* by Marianne Moore, introduced by Eliot, New York, The Macmillan Company, 1935, p. viii.

14. "Religion and Literature", *Selected Essays*, p. 398.

15. *Selected Essays*, p. 334.

16. *The Athenaeum*, 30 May 1919, p. 392.

17. *The Use of Poetry*, p. 143.

18. *Nation and Athenaeum*, XL, No. 19, Feb. 1927, p. 18.

19. "Eliot's stature as critic", *Commentary*, Nov. 1958, p. 400.

20. *Ibid.*

21. *Ibid.*, p. 402.

22. *Ibid.*, p. 408.

23. Eliot's Introduction, *Selected Poems* by Marianne Moore, p. 10.

24. *Ibid.*, p. xi.
25. Eliot's critical note to *Collected Poems* by Harold Monro, London, Cobden Sanderson, p. xiv.
26. *The Use of Poetry*, p. 148.
27. *Ibid.*, p. 144.
28. Eliot's Preface, *English Poetry* by Leone Vivante, Faber & Faber, p. viii.
29. *The Partisan Review, XVI*, Feb. 1949, pp. 119-137.
30. *On Poetry and Poets*, p. 106.

2

Influences on T.S. Eliot

Influences on T.S. Eliot are many and varied — both native and alien, but he has not simply copied or parroted others. Eliot's perspicuous and agile mind has digested the numerous influences — influences were experiences to Eliot — and the result is "those are pearls that were his eyes". His mind was so fine that it compressed everything into unity, system and coherence. We mark the spark of unity rediating from his verse and prose alike. In spite of the multifarious influences, there is an identity of spirit, progression and development rather than confusion in his critical ideas. Had it not been so, Eliot's work would have made dull reading. One can say somewhat in Eliot's vein that a bad critic imitates but what a good critic steals from others he colours with his own personality and weaves in the fabric of his logical feelings.

T.S. Eliot was born in 1888 at 2635 Locust Street in St. Louis, Missouri. He was the seventh and the last issue of his parents. Henry Ware Eliot and Charlotte Champe Stearns were Eliot's father and mother; William Greenleaf Eliot was Eliot's grandfather. The hereditary influence is to be noted in T.S. Eliot. Eliot himself writes :

> The early history of this university [Washington University] which my grandfather served with tireless devotion until his death, is inextricably involved for me in family and personal, history. I never knew my grandfather : he died a year before my birth. But I was brought up to be very much aware of him, so much so that as a child I thought of him as still the head of

the family — a ruler for whom in absentia my grandmother stood as vice-regent. The standard of conduct was that which my grandfather had set; our moral judgments, our decisions between duty and self-indulgence, were taken as if, like Moses, he had brought down the tables of the Law, any deviation from which would be sinful.[1]

The classical trait and the disposition towards order and discipline in T.S. Eliot are to be linked up with the nature and the temperament of Eliot's father and grandfather. William Greenleaf Eliot, Eliot's grandfather, represented the tradition of "astonishing personal purity and moral beauty" and led a life of pure, unfaltering, unflagging endeavour. He wrote fugitive pieces — articles for newspapers; sermons and addresses. His *The Discipline of Sorrow* consisted of studies in consolation after the death of his daughter, Mary. Writers envied him, the literary finish" of everything he composed and business men envied his organising ability. He wrote without adjectives and avoided flights of fancy. He had a particular kind of artistic sensibility which he handed down to his children.

William Greenleaf Eliot had expected that all his sons would, like Thomas Lamb Eliot, follow him and enter the ministry, but ministry was the last thing Henry Ware Eliot wanted. When he told his father that he wanted to go into some active business, his father, in sudden anger, said, "Then your education is wasted." T.S. Eliot was the son of a business man but Eliot's father, like all his brothers, was responsive to the arts. He had some talent for painting. But his taste was conservative. In politics he was staunchly Republican, in all matters conservative. The shrewdness and practical-mindedness of Eliot are to be seen in line with the businessmanship of his father.

Charlotte Champe Stearns graduated at Framingham from the advanced class of 1862. "A young lady of unusual brilliancy as a scholar" — was the testimonial given to her by the institution. She did not take kindly to the stoppage of her education as she intensely desired to continue further studies and grow in fame as a writer. Her desires were not satisfactorily fulfilled. In all her work there are the qualities of a true poet. She was not concerned with rhapsodizing or with colours but with the management of metrics and rhyme. She worked to master a stanza, then passed on to experiment with another. For her son the test of a poet has been the power to innovate. She seldom forced or inflated her language. Her work is clear and quietly passionate.

A writer depends, Eliot wrote in 1917, on the accumulated sensations of the first twenty-one years. His own first seventeen years were spent in St. Louis. William Greenleaf Eliot was critical of St. Louis in the thirties and the forties for its exclusive preoccupation with Mammon. Certainly he knew that moral decay was a possible consequence of wealth. "Money", "business" and "commercialism" were the words used for St. Louis. In Eliot the voice of indignation was first heard in "Burbank....Bleistein" — where the commercial culture of the Midwest is sharply caricatured. Among the phrases is "money in furs". St. Louis had developed out of the riches of fur-trade. But in 1900 St. Louis had its worthier side too. For a generation a movement of artists had made St. Louis famous across the continent as a centre of philosophy and the arts, and in 1900 the legacy of their endeavours still continued.

Having this brighter aspect of St. Louis in mind Eliot said : "I am very well satisfied with having been born in St. Louis : in fact I think I was fortunate to have been born here, rather than in Boston or New York or London."[2]

Eliot entered Harvard in 1906, took his bachelor's degree in 1909, his master's in 1910; spent a year in Paris; and studied for three years at Harvard from 1911 to 1914.

Harvard in Eliot's time was the seat of great learning and wisdom. At the beginning of the present century a number of intellectuals like William James, Santayana, Royce and Babbitt were lecturing and training their students to unfold their own potentiality and versatility. Eliot has condemned England and America in the first part of the twentieth century as intellectual deserts. But he has remembered his individual teachers — above all, Professor Babbitt — with a great reverence and admiration. In the middle twenties Eliot. Selected books by his former teachers for review in the *Times Literary Supplement*. He wrote on

Founders of the Middle Ages, by Dr. E.K. Rand, under whom he had studied Latin, and On *the Renaissance of the Twelfth Century* by Dr. Haskins, whose course on medieval history he had attended. The Widener Library catalogue lists a copy of *What is a Classic?* inscribed by Eliot in 1942, "for Ken Rand with deference". In the review of *Founders Of the Middle* Ages[3] for the *Times Literary Supplement* he described Dr. Rand as one of the foremost living authorities on Boethius and a "scholar of intelligence and wide sympathies." The review of *Founders* concludes by mentioning Dr. Rand "as one of the finest classical scholars and humanists of our time...."

Eliot's debt to Harvard is immense. The university supplied him a reservoir of stimulating ideas.

At the Smith Academy in St. Louis, Eliot began to read Latin at twelve, Greek a year after. He had received a gold medal for the best record in Latin, but Greek had seemed to him "a much more exciting study" : "I still think it a much greater language, a language which has never been surpassed as a vehicle for the fullest range and the finest shades of thought and feeling."[4]

The undergraduates generally avoided the classical courses but Eliot choose to continue Greek and Latin studies at Harvard. Eliot and a fascination of the unpopular and the conservative from the very beginning. Out of the eighteen courses which made up Eliot's undergraduate programme, seven were classical. Eliot has been always defending the study of the classics. In the twenties he wrote, "neglect of Greek means for Europe a relapse into unconscious [ness]." In the thirties, Eliot defended it as a discipline, and added that we should choose not only the subject which appeals to us but also train our sensibility to like what we do not like to study.

When Eliot was taking an undergraduate course at Harvard, George Herbert Palmer was the lecturer in the history of early philosophy. Norman Foerster recalled George Herbert Palmer as a stimulating lecturer :

> ....a fascinating lecturer, one of the best I have heard'
> He made philosophers come alive. First came the
> philosopher the man, then his reasons for departing from

the previous philosopher, then the building up of a new edifice that looked impregnable. Palmer spoke with notes, simply and quietly, with perfect precision, in human language free of technical jargon...."[5]

In the early Dante essay a passage reminds us of Palmer's teaching when Eliot discusses Parmenides and Empedocles.

In the Latin literature course, resumed in the second semester of the academic year 1908-09, Eliot preferred Petronius and Apuleius. In this class Eliot received the gift of Petronius, as the epigraph to *The Waste Land* and the epigraph and allusions in *The Sacred Wood* show. Riviere defines a masterpiece as one which stays in our mind for ever. In Eliot's experience, according to this definition, "Trimalchio's Feast" was a masterpiece. Like certain figures in Ben Jonson and Dickens, Trimalchio demonstrated that a writer may lend his characters power by drawing them with a generous impossibility. If he makes them caricatures, they will radiate (as Eliot wrote in *The Sacred Wood*) " — the kind of power....which comes from below the intellect." Reading Petronius with Professor Clifford H. Moore, Eliot's sense of caricature was strengthened.

Eliot's interest and study of Dante are to be ascribed to a Harvard tradition. Professor Ticknor of Harvard had introduced the study of the Romance languages in 1819; Longfellow had followed; then James Russell Lowell and Charles Eliot Norton. Eliot followed the well-established example. The teachers encouraged their undergraduates, year by year, to go to Dante directly without preliminaries on grammar; and the students after becoming teachers went on reading Dante with the same zest and whole-hearted concentration and absorption. Barrett Wendell has written about the process :

> In my junior year a lecture of Professor Norton excited
> in me a wish to read Dante under Mr. Lowell. I did
> not know a word of Italian though : and I was firmly
> resolved to waste no more time on elementary
> grammar....Mr. Lowell never gave us less than a canto
> to read and often gave us two or three; he never, from
> the beginning, bothered us with 'a particle of linguistic
> irrelevance. Here before us was a great poem — a

lasting expression of what life had meant to a human
being dead and gone these five centuries. Let us try,
as best we might, to see what life had meant to this
man; let us see what relation his experience, great and
small, bore to ours; and now and then, let us pause for
a moment to notice how wonderfully beautiful his
expression of this experience was....That was the spirit
of Mr. Lowell's teaching. It opened to some of us a
new world. In a month I could read Dante better than
I ever learned to read Greek or Latin or German....So
in a single college year, we read through the *Divine
Comedy,* and the *Vita Nuova,* and dipped into the
convex and the lesser writings of Dante. And more than
one of us learned to love them always.[6]

In the Harvard fashion Eliot read Dante before he had any
Italian grammar. He puzzled out the *Divine Comedy* with the help
of a prose translation beside the text....and when I thought I had
grasped the meaning of the passage which specially delighted me,
I committed it to memory; so that, for some years, I was able to
recite a large part of one canto or another to myself, lying in
bed or on a railway journey. Heaven knows what it would have
sounded like, had I recited it aloud; but it was by this means
that I steeped myself in Dante's poetry.[7]

After forty years (he said in 1950) Eliot still regarded Dante's
poetry which, like Shakespeare's, Homer's and Virgil's, grew
more inspiring and communicative to him with the passage of
time, as "the more persistent and deepest influence" upon his
own. Eliot did what Wendell and the other Harvard teachers had
done before him : transmitted his enthusiasm for Dante to a new
generation.   Eliot is of the opinion that the main purpose of
criticism is to rouse curiosity about a work, to send readers to it,
and so to give them an opportunity to share it.

Eliot followed the freshman course in English Literature given
by Dean Briggs, by whom at least one revelation was begun. In
"Donne in our Time" Eliot writes :

Professor Briggs used to read, with great persuasiveness
and charm, *verses of* Donne to the freshmen at
Harvard....I confess that I have not forgotten what
Professor Briggs told us about the poet; but I know

that whatever he said, his own words and his own quotations were enough to attract to private reading, at least one freshman who had already absorbed some of the Elizabethan dramatists, but who had not yet approached the metaphysicals....[8]

Out of the first experiences there grew, not rapidly but after sometime, the famous revolution in Eliot's experience which he communicated to others with great zest and feeling and thus transformed the public taste.

Donne was not unknown before but Eliot did, in fact, revolutionise the appreciation of Donne. Nobody before Eliot had brought Donne and other metaphysicals to bear upon the reader's sensibility with such force. Many critics have pointed out that Eliot did not discover an unknown poet, nor restore a "lost" one. Donne was a living possession of nineteenth century England, as René Wellek has mentioned Coleridge, Saintsbury and Gosse among his admirers. In the second issue of Margret Fuller's *Dial,* October 1840, Donne is named : "How can the age be a bad one which gives me Plato and Paul and Plutarch, Saint Augustine, Spinoza, Chapman....Donne and Sir Thomas Browne, besides its own riches' Charles Eliot Norton was a collector of Donne. In St. Louis, William Marion Ready was printing poems of Donne in the Mirror in 1904. Briggs read Donne to his classes because Donne was one of the possessions of Americans who cared for poetry. What Eliot did was to use Donne creatively and inspire the generation to continue and extend his usage. That was the revolution Eliot brought about, though he did not discover Donne.

There was a teacher at Harvard of singular repute — George Santayana. *The Monthly* wrote in 1912 that he had "attained in Harvard a following which in enthusiasm and intensity, if not in numbers, is almost impossible to parallel : the students were conscious of greatness in his presence, of completeness and grandeur." After taking Palmer's course in ancient philosophy, Eliot followed Santayana's *History of Modern Philosophy.* In his first graduate year, beginning in September 1909, he choose for his study Santayana's more advanced course — "Ideals of Society, Religion, Art and Science in their Historical Development."

Santayana had the gifted power for explaining every philosopher with lucidity and charm. Compelled by the academic fashion of the day to pretend a speciality, he announced that aesthetics was his field and wrote his first book, *The Sense of Beauty*. He had been much influenced by Spinoza, and of him he spoke and wrote with animated admiration. Some of Eliot's very appreciative references to Spinoza remind us of Santayana's teaching or to reading done under his inspiration.

Santayana's statement, "Wisdom comes by disillusionment", had immensely appealed to Eliot. Eliot also acquired the faith that wisdom follows disillusionment and humility. Eliot is appreciative of the "disillusioned" mind of Pascal.

Mrs. Q.D. Leavis recalls in her articles[9], the reference by Mr. Eliot to *Three Philosophical Poets* in the introduction to his Dante hand-book. George Santayana declares in the prologue to his novel that there is "an immense advantage in belonging to the Catholic tradition," and this has kinship with the tradition of Eliot. Mrs. Q.D. Leavis further points out in that very article that the interesting essay "The Absence of Religion in Shakespeare" gives us a clue about some odd remarks in Eliot's *Dante* about Dante being a superior kind of poet to Shakespeare.

The following part of *Three Philosophical Poets* of George Santayana has influenced some of Eliot's statements of Dante :

> Our poets are things of shreds and patches; they give us episodes and studies, a sketch of curiosity, a glimpse of that romance; they have no total vision, no grasp of the whole reality, and consequently no capacity for a sane steady idealization. This age of material elaboration has no sense for perfection. Its fancy is retrospective, whimsical and flickering; its ideals, when it has any, are negative and partial; its moral strength is a blind and miscellaneous vehemence. Its poetry in a word is a poetry of barbarism.[10]

With such poets Santayana contrasts Dante, whom he characterises with words that Eliot may have remembered :

Dante gives us a successful example of the highest species of poetry. His poetry covers the whole field from which poetry may be fetched and to which poetry may be applied, from the inmost recesses of the heart to the uttermost bounds of nature and of destiny....[11]

There is a clear-cut parallelism and similarity of concept between Eliot's idea of objective correlative and one of Santayana's expressions. George Santayana writes :

The substance of poetry is, after all, emotion....Passions are the chief basis, of all interests, even the most ideal, and the passions are seldom brought into play except by contact of man with man. The various forms of love and hate are only possible in society and to imagine occasions in which these feelings may manifest all their inward vitality, is the poet's function. The poet's art is to a great extent, the art of intensifying emotions by assembling the scattered objects that naturally arouse them....The thrilling adventures which the poet craves demand an appropriate theatre; the glorious emotions with which be bubbles over must at all hazards find or feign their correlative objects.[12]

There is another passage in — The Genteel Tradition in American Philosophy" which seems to have influenced the expression of Eliot's review entitled "American Literature." George Santayana writes :

The three American writers whose personal endowment was perhaps the finest — Poe, Hawthorne and Emerson — had all a certain starved abstract quality....They were too keen, too perceptive, and independent for that. But life offered them tittle digestible material, nor were they naturally voracious. They were fastidious, and under the circumstances they were starved. Emerson, to be sure, fed on books....And to feed on books for a philosopher or a poet, is still to starve. Books....cannot supply him with substance, if he is to have any. Therefore, the genius of Poe and Hawthorne, and even of Emerson was employed on a sort of inner play or digestion of vacancy. It was a refined labour, but it was in danger of being morbid or tinkling or self-indulgent. It was a play of intra-mental rhymes. Their mind was like an old music-box, full of tender echoes and quaint fancies. These fancies expressed their personal genius sincerely as drama may....their manner, in a word, was subjective....

And T.S. Eliot in his review deplores in a similar vein the lack of substance and subject-matter in writers like Hawthorne, Poe and Whitman. He also dwells upon what he calls the thinness of their world. Eliot says in that very review that Hawthorne might have been greater that is, more important — had he had a more important subject-matter. Eliot writes :

> Hawthorne, Poe and Whitman are all pathetic creatures; they are none of them so great as they might have been....the originality, if not the full mental capability of these men was brought out, forced out, by the starved environment....What the Americans, in point of fact, did suffer from was the defect of society in a larger sense....their world was thin; it was not corrupt enough, worst of all it was second-hand; it was not original and self-dependent it was a shadow. Poe and Whitman, like bulbs in a glass bottle, could only exhaust what was in them....[14]

When Eliot entered Harvard, its president C.W. Eliot, a third cousin, was to have the end of his term of office after a short period. It had been a remarkable term. C.W. Eliot preferred the practice of the "elective system" at Harvard. It is the system that is even to-day found in most American universities. It extends a right to the undergraduates to pursue or to leave the old discipline. It brings a wide range of subjects at their disposal. It is a reflection of the democratic doctrine that anybody can make his choice according to his sweet will.

After vacating the presidency in 1909, C.W. Eliot appeared before Harvard Summer School of Theology to enunciate the seven propositions of the "Religion of the Future" :

1. The religion of the future will not be based on authority, either spiritual or temporal, for the tendency towards liberty is progressive and among educated men is irresistible.

2. ....

3. No worship, expressed or implied, of dead ancestors, teachers or rules.

4. The primary object will not be personal welfare or safety of the individual....but....service to the others.

5. It will not be propitiatory, sacrificial or expiatory.

6. It will not perpetuate the Hebrew anthropomorphic representation of God.

7. It will not be gloomy, ascetic or maledictory.

T.S. Eliot was attending the Harvard Summer School that year when this new revelation burst upon the public mind. T.S. Eliot was on the side of the President's critics. He differed from the President on almost every public issue. He was sharply critical of the emphasis of the University administrators on numbers and size; be attacked the "elective system :"

> No one can become really educated without having pursued some study in which he took no interest for it is a part of education to learn to interest ourselves in subjects for which we have no aptitude.[15]

Eliot meant that a student should study Latin and Greek whether be liked them or not. He deplores the "elective system" of C.W. Eliot as the corollary of democracy. His opinion is that "natural and unregenerate man", left free to choose, is liable to make the wrong choice. His conception of religion is the reverse of the President's "religion of the future", and depends on authority and tradition, on a Johnsonian sense of the terror of death.

Eliot opposed the assumption of C.W. Eliot as Irving Babbitt and Barrett Wendell did. Barrett Wendell once asked Professor Merriman : "In all the twentyfive years you have known me, Roger, have you ever heard me utter one liberal sentiment ?" Merriman : "None, Sir." Wendell : "Thank God."

Wendell's onslaught and vehemence against the assumptions of his time foreshadow, in their arguments and turns of phrase, some of the editorial commentaries in Eliot's *Criterion*. Wendell writes in 1913 :

> We are living in an age of less liberty; every extension of suffrage makes the individual less free. Such bonds diminish all sense of responsibility. It was evil that many were once slaves of few, if you will. It is worse evil that now we are bidden to believe that — all should be the slaves of majorities — whatever their whims....[16]

Eliot's early commentaries, compared to those of Wendell, lack cheer, and are tight-lipped. In April 1924 Eliot expressed his hatred for modern politics with "their meanness of spirit, that egotism of motive, that incapacity for surrender or allegiance to something outside of oneself". Eliot once sharply attacked a British General Election, that of 1929, as a "waste of time, money, energy and illusion". Eliot thinks again and returns to the attack more gaily in "Second Thoughts on the Brainless Election : "

> The Labour Party is a capitalist party in the sense that it is living on the reputation of the thinking done by the Fabians of a generation ago. The names of a few men of brains still lend it a sunset glory. The Conservative Party has a great opportunity, in the fact that within the memory of no living man under sixty has it acknowledged any contact with intelligence....

In the first three years at Harvard Eliot was not any distinguished figure. Reading undergradute journals of the time one does not encounter his name often except in the *Advocate*. William Chase Greene writes : "He was recognised as able and witty; not influential,' at the time; rather aloof and silent; I used to tell him he reminded me of a smiling and quizzical figure of Buddha."

In December 1908, Eliot had made a revelatory discovery, by picking up, in the Library on the Harvard Union, Arthur Symons' book, *The Symbolist Movement in Literature.* He has fully acknowledged his indebtedness to it, most outspokenly in *The Criterion of* January 1930, when he reviewed Peter Quennell's *Baudelaire and the* Symbolists :

> Mr. Quennell has done for his generation what Arthur Symons did many years ago with his *Symbolist movement in Literature.* I am not disposed to disparage Mr. Symons' book; it was a very good book for its time, it did make the reader want to read the poets Mr. Symons wrote about, I myself owe Mr. Symons a great debt; but for having read his book, I should not, in 'the year 1908, have heard of Laforgue or Rimbaud; I should probably not have begun to read Verlaine; and but for reading Verlaine, I should not have heard of Corbiére. So the Symons' book is one of those which have affected the course of my life....[17]

And through Eliot the book affected the course of English poetry and criticism.

Eliot was influenced by the French Symbolists both in his verse and critical ideas. Edmund Wilson has rightly pointed out : "But it is from the conversational-ironic, rather than from the serious-aesthetic, tradition of Symbolism that T.S. Eliot derives. Corbiére and Laforgue are almost everywhere in his early work."[18] The conversational-ironic note pervades not only Eliot's verse but also his prose. The critical essays of Eliot have often an ironic flavour, full of turns and twists. Irony is a great weapon with Eliot which he wields with softness and subtlety. The "serious-aesthetic tradition" of Symbolism has its impact on Eliot's theory of poetry. Eliot's insistence on the making, pruning and shaping of a poem and differentiation of art-emotion from crude emotion, and predilection for the perfection of the language, rhythm and structure, and concern for technique and fastidious craftsmanship have the marked flavour of the Symbolists. Eliot's "superior amusement" is the refined form of "art for art's sake." The Symbolists rejected sociological and ethical themes, insisting that art pursues the sensation of beauty apart from moral or social responsibility. In short, they subscribed to the doctrine of "art for art's sake." The line of the primary influence of the Symbolists runs from Poe to Baudelaire and to Mallarmé. Poe defined a poem as "rhythmic creation of beauty." T.S. Eliot writes about the birth and origin of the poem in a somewhat similar vein :

For other poets — at least, for some other poets — the poem may begin to shape itself in fragments of musical rhythm, and its structure will first appear in terms of something analogous to musical form....[19]

And in another place :

I think that a poet may gain much from the study of music....but I know that a poem or a passage of a poem, may tend to realize itself first as a particular rhythm before it reaches expression in words, and that this rhythm may bring to birth the idea and the image; and I do not believe that this is an experience peculiar to myself.[20]

Above all, Arthur Symons' book set Eliot on the way to Laforgue. Eliot has mentioned more than once the prominent part Laforgue played in his development. In a talk given at the Italian Institute in London in 1950, Eliot said :

> Such early influences, the influences, so to speak, that first introduce one to oneself, are, I think, due to an impression which is, in one aspect, the recognition of a temperament akin to one's own and another aspect the discovery of form of expression which gives a clue to the discovery of one's own form. These are not two things but two aspects of the same thing.

At another place :

It is true that I owed, and have always acknowledged, an equally great debt to certain French poets of the late 19th century, about whom I have never written. I have written about Baudelaire, but nothing about Jules Laforgue, to whom I owe more than to any one poet in any language, or about Tristan Corbiérc, to whom I owe something else. The reason, I believe, is that none commissioned me to do so....[21]

With the incentive from Symons' book Eliot went, in December 1908, or New Year 1909, to Schoenhof's and put an order for the three volumes of Laforgue. He got absorbed in the study of the French symbolists. Eliot had noted Arthur Symons' observation on the "asentimentalism" of Laforgue, in whose art "sentiment is squeezed out of the word before one begins to play ball with it." Eliot realized that Laforgue had used certain metropolitan sensations beautifully and like him he incorporated the metropolitan vision into his poetry.

Eliot had certainly, according to E.J.H. Greene's book, read Baudelaire in 1907 and had come across his compelling images of the city. Eliot recalls in 1950 in his address — "What Dante Means to Me" his debt to Baudelarie :

> I think that from Baudelaire I learned first a precedent for the poetical possibilities never developed by any poet writing in my own language, of the more sordid aspects of the modern metropolis, of the possibility of fusion between the sordidly realistic and the phantasmagoric, the possibility of the juxtaposition of the

matter of fact and the fantastic, From him, as from
Laforgue, I learned that the sort of material that I had,
the sort of experience that an adolesent had in an
industrial city in America, could be the material for
poetry; and that the source of new poetry might be
found in what had been regarded hitherto as the
impossible, the sterile, the intractably unpoetic. That,
in fact, the business of the poet was to make poetry
out of the unexplored resources of the unpoetical : that
the poet, in fact, was committed by his profession to
turn the unpoetical into poetry. A great poet can give
a younger poet everything that he has to give him, in
a very few lines.[22]

This is high praise accorded to Baudelaire. Baudelaire, as Eliot
says, invented a language when French poetry in particular was
famishing for such invention. And this is enough, as Eliot
continues, to make of Baudelaire a great poet, a landmark in
poetry. Baudelaire, Eliot points out, gave new possibilities to
poetry in a new stock of imagery of contemporary life. His
language introduces something new and something universal in
modern life. It is not merely in the use of imagery of common
and sordid life of a great metropolis, but in the elevation of such
imagery to the first intensity — presenting it as it is and yet
making it represent something much more than itself, and this
way Baudelaire has created a mode of release and expression for
other men. From the imagery and language of Baudelaire, Eliot
found a general clue to writing poetry in the twentieth century
of immense panorama, futility and anarchy, and machine rhythms.
Hence, Eliot rightly asserts in his critical essays that the idiom
and the language of every generation cannot be the same as those
of the past: they must change and catch the rhythm of the
conditions and the language of the people of their time. This is
the universal law of poetry; and one must explore new avenues
and new possibilities for poetry in every age. Eliot compares the
evening spread out against the sky to a patient etherised upon
the table, and Wordsworth compared evening to a nun breathless
with adoration, but Eliot is no less beautiful or poetical than
Wordsworth in his expression.

Baudelaire has had his impact upon T.S. Eliot not only by

his new language and the new imagery of the metropolis but
also by his attitude to life. Eliot means to say that Baudelaire
may not be a Christian but supremely tends towards Christianity
and divinity. That is why Eliot says that Baudelaire's renovation
of an attitude towards life is "no less radical and no less
important". Baudelaire enters Christianity by the back-door. He
communicates to Eliot and to others the knowledge and the sense
of good and evil. He was at least capable of damnation denied
to the politicians and the newspaper editors.

Eliot says that Baudelaire was one of those who have great
strength, but strength merely to suffer. And such suffering as
Baudelaire's implies the possibility of a positive state of beatitude.
Indeed, in his way of suffering, Eliot continues, there is already
a kind of presence of the supernatural and of the superhuman.
Eliot finds in Baudelaire a point of radical importance for himself
as well as for the twentieth century confronted with immense
futility : Baudelaire rejects always the purely natural and purely
human; in other words, he is neither a "naturalist" nor a —
humanist". Eliot writes :

> What is significant about Baudelaire is his theological
> innocence. He is discovering Christianity for himself,
> be is not assuming it as a fashion or weighing social
> or political reasons or any other accidents....His
> Christianity is rudimentary or embryonic....His business
> was not to practise Christianity, but....what was much
> more important for his time, to assert its necessity.[23]

Eliot finds some common factors in Baudelaire, T.E. Hulme
and Pascal. At the end of his essay on Baudelaire, Eliot quotes a
paragraph of T.E. Hulme, which Eliot says, Baudelaire would
have approved.

One point of Eliot's wrangle with Arnold is the fact that
Arnold presents literature as a substitute for religion. Eliot is of
firm opinion that nothing can be a substitute for anything else.
Eliot writes : "....Literature or culture, tended with Arnold to usurp
the place of Religion."[24]

To present something as a substitute for religion is to petrify
it, mutilate, or to minimize it. To associate literature with religion
is also to bring impurity and confusion in literature. Eliot's

dissatisfaction with the "religion" of Arnold is that it is not religious enough. Besides, Arnold's religion has only an enthusiastic, humanistic, sentimental air, and this cannot be palatable to Eliot.

Eliot was appointed to the Board of Editors of the *Advocate* in January 1909, It was an *Advocate* policy to review the publications of literary figures. Such a publication called *The Wine of the Puritans* by Van Wyck Brooks appeared in the spring of 1909 and Eliot reviewed it. This book was significant to a man who had recently discovered the French Symbolists and was assimilating their poetry of dinginess. Brooks confirmed that the artist needed the seediness, the ugliness of contemporary life.

During the two terms 1909-10, Eliot completed the work for a Master's degree in English literature with all-round distinction. To read the list of his courses is to be acquainted with much of the facts. Among the courses taken by T.S. Eliot was Babbitt's French. Babbitt was all muscle and force but preached the ordered control of energy. Paul Elmer More was Babbitt's fellow-student.

Eliot recalls his debt to Babbitt much later in his convocation lecture delivered at the University of Leeds in July 1961, where he, apprises us of other facts also :

> My old teacher and master, Irving Babbitt, to whom I owe so much, stopped on his way back to Harvard from Paris, where he had been lecturing, and he and Mrs. Babbitt dined with me. I had not seen Babbitt for some years, and I felt obliged to acquaint him with a fact as yet unknown to my small circle of readers (for this was I think in the year 1927) that I had been recently baptized and confirmed into the Church of England. I knew that it would come as a shock to him to learn that any disciple of his had so turned his coat, though he had already had what must have been a much greater shock when his close friend and ally Paul Elmer More defected from Humanism to Christianity. But all Babbitt said was : "I think you should come out into the open...."[25]

Literature and the American College, which Eliot knew as an important book, was published by Houghton Mifflin in 1908. The subtitle of the book was "Essays in Defence of the

Humanities" by showing how the Romans fell into misuse of it and were recalled to order by Aulus Gellius. "Humanitas," says Gellius, "is incorrectly used to denote a 'promiscuous benevolence', what the Greeks call philanthropy', whereas the word really implies doctrine and discipline, and is applicable not to men in general but only to a select few — it is in short aristocratic and not democratic in its implication."[26]

Babbitt denounced the quest for size, the criterion of numbers, quick industrialisation, the emphasis on wealth. He wrote: "We [in America] seem certain to break all records of bigness, but unless that bigness is tempered by quality, we shall sprawl helplessly in the midst of our accumulated wealth and power, or at best arrive at a sort of senseless iteration."[27] Eliot reproached contemporary society for the quantitative life adulterated with moral impressionism.

John Jay Chapman and Babbitt attacked the prevailing ideology of the adoption of the mores of industry and concentration on size. They were isolated in their stand, but the students were on their side. Eliot writes about Babbitt : "His outspoken contempt for methods of teaching in vogue had given him a reputation for unpopularity which attracted to him some discerning graduates and undergraduates."

Eliot was fascinated by Babbitt's assault on the popular. Later on, he championed Joyce and Wyndham Lewis for their acceptance of unpopularity. Babbitt's thesis in *Literature and the American College* centres mainly in reactions against over-concern for buildings and numbers and the weakening of discipline in modern education. Eliot came to Babbitt in a receptive year and read in his book the doctrine of classicism and the supplementary doctrine of tradition.

Babbitt prescribed the study of Greek and the Greeks if one wanted to know how to write or judge writing. Their work, he said, was judicious, moderate and humane. *Literature and the American College* is, in fact, a primary document of the neo-classical movement in English. In 1908 Babbitt spoke for the cultivation of the classical spirit : "The classical spirit, in its purest form, feels itself consecrated to the service of a high impersonal reason. Hence its sentiment of restraint and discipline, its sense of proportion and pervading law."

Eliot's response can be illustrated by a passage in *The Criterion* in January 1926; explaining the classicism for which his periodical stood, he said that this did not mean that living art should be measured by dead laws, but it meant that "there is a tendency discernible even in art — towards a higher and clearer conception of reason, and a more severe and serene control of emotions by reason." Here Babbitt's voice is present in Eliot's.

But a service almost equally significant was to introduce Eliot to the theory of the living past. Babbitt disliked the overrating of originality. His famous attack on Rousseau centred on the charge that he bad overvalued his differences from other men. The excellence of Greek literature lay in — "the balance it maintained between the forces of tradition and the claims of originality...." The Greeks hoped — "to become original by assimilating tradition." "There is needed in the classics to-day," Babbitt decided, "a man who can understand the past with the result, not of loosening, but of strengthening his grasp upon the present." Eliot soon welcomed the work of Ezra Pound because he found him such a man, when be reviewed *Quia Pauper Amavi* in 1919 :

> Mr. Pound proceeds by acquiring the entire past ; and when the entire past is acquired, the constituents fall into place and the present is revealed. Such a method involves immense capacities of expressing oneself through historical masks. Mr. Pound has a unique gift for expression through some phase of past life. This is not archaeology or pedantry, but one method, and a very high method, of poetry.[28]

"Tradition and the Individual Talent" appeared in the *Egoist* almost at the same date. That essay was the synthetic whole of Babbitt's traditionalism and the traditionalism of Maurras.

When Eliot was Babbit's pupil, the crucial American debate, whether the nation's art should be utterly independent or whether it should grow from the traditions of Europe, was already seventy years old. James Russell Lowell was devoted to tradition. Babbitt had absorbed Lowell's teaching. Eliot received the lesson from

Babbitt and systematised his own theory of tradition, and demonstrated it in his poetry and criticism.

Besides his other debt to Babbitt, Eliot learnt from him the art of controversy. Babbitt and Eliot both impress us by their systematic method and in their essays we feel that we are watching reason in action.

Eliot said in 1926 that Babbitt's book *Democracy and Leadership* highlighted the severe and serene classical spirit. In discipline, restraint and order, Eliot excels Babbitt, and excels him most in the method learnt from him.

When the professorship of English Literature at Oxford fell vacant in 1922 on the death of Sir Walter Raleigh, Eliot suggested in his "London Letter" to the *Dial* that Babbitt would be a good successor. In the later twenties Eliot disagreed with the humanist's allegiance to "ethical will" as against his own faith in revealed Christianity. Some of the criticism of Humanism Eliot wrote himself, with the result that Babbitt complained : "He begins his letters 'Dear Master', but he attacks me whenever he writes about me." Eliot cannot be held to have attacked him; he simply disputed and argued with his teacher.

Babbitt helped Eliot in imbibing and strengthening the sense of authority, the sense of tradition, and disgust at the excess of naturalism and Rousseauism. The books of Babbitt have been thought-provoking to Eliot and to others. *In Rousseau and Romanticism,* Professor Babbitt studies Rousseau less in himself than as the most important single figure in a great international movement extending from the eighteenth century to the present day. The type of romanticism to which he devotes his full attention is only the emotional aspect of naturalism, and the final question raised is the value of a naturalistic view of life. The present naturalistic excess is, he holds, a menace to civilization. Babbitt seeks remedy in a positive and critical humanism, Eliot in Catholicism and classicism.

According to Babbitt, as we find in *Rousseau and Romanticism* (1919) and *Democracy and Leadership* (1924), the modern age had carried the revolt against authority a rebellion instigated by Rousseau — to the point of chaos. The romantic stress on personality had led to a denial of all absolutes and positive values; self-expression had become the norm — the only norm. What was needed, in life as well as in literature, was a return to ethical imperatives. But Eliot firmly believed that the Humanism of Babbitt, however, critical and positive, cannot work for long unless it has its roots in the soil of a Pascal, or a Baudelaire.

Eliot argues that Babbitt is unable to take the religious view-that is to say, he cannot accept any dogma or revelation ; and considers humanism as the alternative to religion. This alternative is no more than a substitute for religion, and it is erroneous to think otherwise.

"I suspect," says Eliot, "Mr. Babbitt at times of an instinctive dread of organised religion, a dread that should cramp and deform the free operations of his own mind. If so, he is surely under a misapprehension.²⁹"

Eliot is right in his stand regarding his criticism on the Humanism of Babbitt. He has rightly found out that , there is only a difference of degree between the Humanism of Babbitt and the emotional and romantic Humanism or Naturalism represented by Rousseau and others. One can rightly point out to the defenders of Babbitt : if "reason" and "inner" "check" could have endowed upon man and the world sanity, order and propriety, there would have been no need of human law, organisation and government, and man would have remained quite happy in the state of nature or in the pre-political era. The realisation of the supernatural force of an Almighty Father or religion of one kind or other is a necessity for the sanity, order and health of humanity.

Eliot in his essay, "Second Thoughts about Humanism", quotes from T.E. Hulme in support of his argument against Mr. Babbit :

> I hold the religious Conception of ultimate values to be right, the humanist wrong. From the nature of things, these categories are not inevitable, like the categories of time and space but are *equally objective*. In speaking of religion, it is to this level of abstraction that I wish to refer. I have none of the feeling of *nostalgia*....which

seems to animate most modern defenders of religion. All that seems to me to be bosh. What is important is what nobody seems to realise — the dogmas like that of Original Sin, which are the closest expressions of the categories of the religious attitude that man is in no sense perfect, but a wretched creature, who can yet apprehend perfection. It is not, then, that I put up with the dogmas for the sake of the sentiment, but that I may possibly swallow the sentiment for the sake of dogma.[30]

By the spring of 1910, however, Eliot had planned to spend the coming academic year in Paris. He wanted to study the particular genius of France. Mr. Herbert Howarth says, "A whole book should be written on Eliot's debt, which is a debt of all of us, to the Paris of the five years before the Great War. When that book is written, a considerable chapter will belong to Bergson.

This topic I am not equipped to touch....Only in passing I will quote, as an indication of Bergson's impact of the young people who flocked to hear him at the College de Frace. a passage from Camille Vettard."[31]

Eliot the critic has been influenced[32] by Bergson's account of time, change and individual consciousness. Eliot's remarks about intuition provide probably the best opening to a consideration of Eliot's debt to Bergson. Eliot states in appreciation that Keats' sayings about poetry "keep pretty close to intuition"[33] and he describes wisdom as 'a native gift of intuition' necessary for "understanding the nature of things, certainly of living things, most certainly of the human heart.' "Living" is the key word for understanding in terms of Bergson. Bergson argues that the intellect, capable of generalising and classifying. can only deal adeqately, with inert matter; the living (and it is most concentrated, as it were, in the human heart), which is essentially individual, unique and unrepeatable, can only be known intuitively.

Such a remark by Eliot should not be treated as accidental; it reflects a major trend in Eliot's thinking and this can be best illustrated, as Mr. Philip Le Brun argues, by an examination of a prose dialogue, "Eeldrop and Appleplex", which appeared in 1917 in two parts in the May and September numbers of *The Little*

Review. This little-known piece shows, in a most transparent fashion, the extent to which Bergson did affect Eliot and the ideas it contains lead directly to Eliot's more familiar statements about poetry and poets.

"Eeldrop", who is learned in theology, and Appleplex, a student of the physical and biological sciences, have left for a time their usual social environment in an endeavour to escape "the too well-pigeon-holed, too taken-for-granted, too highly systematized areas and in the language of those whom they sought to aviod — they wish to apprehend the human soul in its concrete individuality."

Whether we call this activity intuition or pure observation hardly matters. Only by escaping the classified and systematized can we grasp what is living.

Eliot, in fact, accepts Bergson's insistence on the connection between life and change. Bergson says in Time and Free Will : "And to be living is to be constantly changing."

And Eliot writes almost in similar rein in 1940. "A living language is constantly changing", and in 1953 he states that "a living literature is always is process of change and for its continuance, the language should be in constant change. If it is changing, it is alive."[34] In "Tradition and the Individual Talent" Eliot declares that the poet must be consious of "what is already living."

The fact is that Eliot's concept of permanence is essentially organic; it is in terms of continuity within time and change and not in terms of something outside time. Eliot was well aware that such a theory of continuity is a part of Bergson's account of the nature of time. The relation between this idea of time as organic development, forming constant and constantly changing patterns and Eliot's theory of tradition must be fairly obivious. Eliot declares in Bergson's vein that the studies in the ballad and in the origin of poetry "have fostered in us the sense of flux and evolution."[35]

Bergson presents the organic concept of time and consciousness. Reviewing a book by Peter Quennell on the Symbolists, Eliot wrote :

When we get to Laforgue we find a poet who seems to express more clearly even than Baudelaire the difficulties of his own age: he speaks to my generation, more intimately than Baudelaire seemed to do. Only later we conclude that Laforgue's present is a narrower present than Baudelairs's and Baudelaire's present extends to more of the past and more of the future.

Eliot describes the artist as "the most conscious of men" because he is able to see below the stratifications of civilization to the savage and the primitive origins which are still present.

In poetry, as Eliot says, there is a "sinking to the most primitive and forgotten." Bergson says that in a stirring drama it seems as if an "appeal had been made within us to certain ancestral memories belonging to a far away past."

Bergson declares that "an idea which is truly ours fills the whole of ourselves"; hence, the idea will take the colour and imprint of feelings.

Bergson argues that a synthesis regflecting the real complex wholeness of consciouness is weakened by "ideas which we receive readymade". Such ideas are not "properly assimilated" and they tend to form a "thick crust which will cover up our own sentiments". Bergson sees this happening in an education which is not properly assimilated. "The feeling of Massinger", Eliot says, is "simple and over-laid with received ideas." In Blake, Eliot finds "one illustration of the eternal struggle of art against education" by which he means "the ordinary processes of society which constitute education for the ordinary man." Eliot writes further :

For the process consists largely in the adquisition of impersonal ideas which obscure what we really are and feel, what we really want, and what really excites our interest. It is of course not the actual information acquired, but the conformity which the accumulation of knowledge is apt to impose, that is harmful. Tennyson is a very fair example of a poet almost wholly encrusted with parasitic opinion, almost wholly merged into his environment.[36]

In the passage where Bergson refers to ideas that are "readymade" and "unassimilated", he suggests that those ideas ,float on the surface" of the mind "like dead leaves." In "Observations on Contemporary Poetry," Eliot says that Laforgue has "unassimilated fragments of metaphysics....floating about." Marianne Moore is always praised by Eliot for being "intensely personal."[37]

In the pages of *Comedy* Bergson alludes to the need for action and "practical simplification" but he points out that they cut us off from "direct contact with sense and consciousness."

Regarding Wyndham Lewis' *Tarr* Eliot says that there is a "direct contact with the senses; perception of the world of immediate experience with its own scale of values."

In *The Sacred Wood* (p. 58) Eliot says that a work of art is a concentration of a great number of experiences which to the practical and active person would not seem to be experiences at all. In *The Use of Poetry* (p. 155) Eliot writes that our lives are mostly constant evasion of ourselves and an evasion of the visible and the sensible world.

Eliot decides that Swift's art is of a higher kind than Johnson's because it "came out of deeper and intenser emotion" and because we feel in it the personality of the creator.

Eliot examines the Elizabethan dramatists especially John Ford from the viewpoint of personality and finds the defect of excessive personality in John Ford. Bergson in *Comedy* (p. 169) says that the art which contains nothing of the personality of the artist, can settle only on the surface of life and society.

Eliot finds in Rimbaud's *Illuminations* "evident sincerity (as if rising immediately and unreflectingly from the core of man's feelings)."[38]

Eliot's term "sincerity"[39] (it is employed by Bergson in *Comedy)* and its opposition to a deliberate and reflective art must appear startling to anyone who takes his antiromantic protestations seriously or his theory of impersonality at its face value.

Eliot remarks that Donne's. conversational tone is closely allied to what we call "sincerity" in poetry.

Eliot states in "Tradition and the Individual Talent" that an artist's experiences do not come "consciously or out of deliberation". Eliot's talk of poetry as an "escape from personality" has much in common with Bergson's idea that art gets rid of "these customary incessant changes which ordinary life brings us back without ceasing to a consciousness of our personality"[40]

Personality in the state of ordinary life and practical actions loses its complexity, fullness and depth; and integration of thought, feeling and sensation becomes impossible. Impersonality means an escape from the limited, divided, social personality (Richards defines impersonality in this way). Of course, the art which reflects personality in this "deeper sense" may not appear to have much relation to the poet's personality, as we know it; this art may constantly surprise us.

"Sincerity" is a kind of artistic integrity, it prevents the artist from tampering with the integral movement of consciousness, forcing him to try to present that movement in all its fullness and complexity.

Eliot was so fascinated by the lectures of Bergson that he would reach the venue, sometimes, even one and a half hours earlier than the scheduled time.[41]

Eliot's belief in "different levels of consciousness" shows a remarkable affinity with the Bergsonian conception of *duriée.*

In Paris Eliot went to Alain-Fournier to learn French conversation. Fournier and his brother-in-law, Jacques Riviére, were an index to the taste of young Frenchmen of the same age as Eliot; and Fournier spoke of his literary interests to Eliot in conversational exchanges.

Fournier's conception of the "*impression sentie*" was very close to Eliot's later conception of the transparent style. In a lecture at New Heaven in 1933, Eliot said that he had "long aimed" at transparency :

> To write poetry....so transparent that we should not see the poetry, but that which we are meant to see through the poetry, poetry so transparent that in reading it we are intent on what the poem points at, and not on the poetry.

In 1932 Eliot wrote a preface to an English translation of *Bubu de Montparnasse,* a novel by Charles-Louis Philippe, which he had read in France in 1910. As he recalled it after twenty-two years, he found its excellence in its *impressions senties*.

Eliot returned to America on the completion of his year, and in September 1911 went back to Harvard beginning the preparatory work for his doctoral thesis. To keep in touch with the French, Eliot subscribed to the *N.R.F.*

At that time the articles of Charles Maurras in *N.R.F.* were very significant to Eliot, who had encountered Charles Maurras's work in 1910. Eliot himself recalled later :

> ....There were then two influences which are not
> incongruous as might at first sight appear; that of I.
> Babbitt and that of Ezra Pound. The influence of Pound
> at that time may be detected in references to Rémy de
> Gourmont, in my papers on Henry James, an author
> whom Pound much admired, but for whom my own
> enthusiasm has somewhat flagged....The influence of
> Babbitt (with an inclusion later of T.E. Hulme and of
> the more literary essays of Charles Maurras) is apparent
> in my recurrent theme of classicism *versus*
> Romanticism."[42]

Charles Maurras was a fierce critic of the nineteenth century and looked back with regret to the order and harmony of the France of the sixteenth and seventeenth centuries. He was possessed by a great image of Europe's civilizing tradition.

In 1926 Eliot called *L,Avenir de l'intelligence of* Charles Maurras an example of the classical spirit in full play. Charles Maurras in this book of 1905 gave a terrifying picture of the human mind reduced to total servility if the trends of the nineteenth century continued. A counter-revolution as advocated by him within the book might bring about a fourth *moment privilegie,* a successor of the perfect moments of Greece, Rome and classical France. His doctrine of the *moment privilegie* was adopted by Eliot. For years together Eliot continued reading Maurras and elaborating and amplifying his thoughts in *The Criterion.*

The author of the *N.R.F.* study of 1913 was Albert Thibaudet. He was by birth a Burgundian and by profession a teacher of philosophy. Thibaudet interpreted Maurras' "aesthetic of the three traditions". There was attached to Maurras' article, in an editorial footnote, a formulation of the three traditions as "classique", "catholique", "monarchique", pointing to Eliot's famous description of himself, in 1928, as a classicist in art, Anglican in religion, and Royalist in politics.

Julien Benda was often wrong but even when he was wrong he was noteworthy and magnificent. His diamond attitude,[43] hard and clear, attracted Eliot. Eliot was always fascinated by the noncompromisers of his time : Babbitt, the quixotic Pound, truculent Wyndham Lewis, the lonely and self-assured Joyce and Benda.

Eliot praised the "formal beauty" of Benda's work. Benda's paragraphs are terse, pure; reading them one has the realization of the rational, intellectual aesthetic which they advocate. Eliot gives Pound credit for making Benda known to the Anglo-Saxon world.

Belphegor by Benda appeared in 1918. Recalling it ten years later, Eliot remembered how "some of us recognized [it] as an art and artist." He praised it in *The Criterion* of January 1926 as one of the living examples of the trend towards classicism.

In the more polemical essays of *The Sacred Wood* one finds the spirit of Benda. But it is not yet well-assimilated. A phrase in which Eliot tries to define Benda's role is not satisfactory : "He is the ideal scavenger of the rubbish of his time." The noun "rubbish" is not the right word. Though Beada is ruthless, he knows the beauty of some of the work he sweeps away. He is really not the scavenger but a surgeon. Eliot in due course was to play the same role. The first thing Eliot acquired from Benda was the ,"art of assassination", and this helped him to down the opposition and initiate literary revolution round about 1920.

Eliot came back to Harvard in September 1911 and got himself enrolled in Lanman's Indic philology course. Babbitt and Paul Elmer More had followed it seventeen years earlier.

Charles Rockwell Lanman, born in 1860, had learned Sanskrit at Yale under William D. Wight Whitney. For two years Eliot studied the language in Latiman's library and during the second year he read Indian philosophy, particularly the Yoga system of Patanjali, under the guidance of James Haughton Woods.

After the spring of 1913 Eliot withdrew from the Sanskrit

courses. He turned to the study of European philosophy. In June 1913 he purchased a copy of F.H. Bradley's *Appearance and Reality* at the Coope in Harvard Square.

At Harvard Eliot must have been aware of Royce, the Professor of History. "The extraordinary philosopher", he subsequently called Royce. In 1908 Royce published his *Philosophy of Loyalty*. The philosophy of loyalty depended on a philosophy of the community.

> "Loyalty....is the willing and thoroughgoing devotion of a self to a cause, when the cause is something which unites many selves in one and which is therefore the interest of the community. For a loyal human being the interest of the community to which he belongs is superior to every merely individual interest of his own.

The individual should find himself in subordination to the community. Passages in Eliot's prose indicate that he was impressed by Royce's doctrine. For example a sentence in *The Sacred Wood* — "the mind of Europe the mind of his own country — a mind which he [the poet] learns in time to be much more important than his own private mind" — reminds us of Royce.

Eliot completed his doctoral thesis on Bradley in April 1916. F.H. Bradley has deeply influenced his critical ideas. Eliot himself has mentioned F.H. Bradley among his masters. Eliot's admiration for the writings of F.H. Bradley has been known ever since he quoted that philosopher in the notes to *The Waste Land*. "The Unity of Experience" constitutes the matrix of Eliot's critical dialectic and Eliot's concept of poetry as "unified sensibility" has the direct bearing of Bradleyan dialectic. Mr. Hugh Kenner, too, has rightly pointed out that "sensibility" is Eliot's term for a scrupulous responsiveness to the Bradleyan immediate experience : a responsiveness that precedes, underlies and contains any degree of analysis.

Eliot is eager thut poetry should register the whole of human sensibility, and the whole of human sensibility is equal to emotion plus intellect or passions plus reasoning. Even in a passionate love-lyric, the witty sardonic laughter and the tone of levity will not mar, rather it will enrich the poem and add a tough reasonableness to it. Eliot finds that a typical metaphysical poem of the English seventeenth century is an attempt to render the whole of sensibility : thought and emotion both are implicit in the metaphysical poems of John Donne. In the "immediate experience" of F.H. Bradley both emotion and reasoning remain in non — relational unity. F.H. Bradley insists on "immediate experience" for the Absolute Reality and Eliot has a similar idea regarding rendering the whole of sensibility in a poem in order to represent the fullest reality. One of the reasons for Eliot's dissatisfaction with English nineteenth century poetry is that this poetry does not render and exploit the whole range of human sensibility. F.H. Bradley seeks the Absolute Reality in the Immediate Experience, and Eliot is earnest to catch the full reality in a poem by translating and registering the whole of sensibility and all the various moods of man. Eliot admires a poem that is simultaneously sympathetic and ironical, sentimental and cynical. When a poet is unable to transmit the whole of sensibility in his own poem, this means that his poem will suffer from "dissociation of sensibility". In this way one can well refer Eliot's term "dissociation of sensibility" back to F.H. Bradley's Immediate Experience.

It is very Bradleyan on the part of Eliot to argue that "the whole of Shakespeare's work is one poem;" so that what is the whole man is not simply his greatest or maturest achievement, but the whole pattern formed by the sequence of plays.

One of the most important deposits of Bradleyism in Eliot's sensibility is visible in the disarmingly hesitant and fragmentary way in which Eliot makes a point or expresses a conviction, doubting that he is quite the man to undertake the job in hand.

Hugh Kenner explains :

> In 1927 he [Eliot] wrote for the *Times Literary Supplement* a tribute to Bradley's greatness disguised as a review of the reprinted *Ethical Studies*; the reference to Bradley's polemical irony and his obvious zest in using it, his habit of discomfiting an opponent with a sudden profession of inability to understand, or incapacity for abstruse thought, suggests a model for some of the polemic gestures of the critic who scored a point against Shelley by claiming not to understand some stanzas from "To a Skylark"....[44]

Mrs. Valerie Eliot has also observed[45] that her husband's prose style was formed very closely on that of Bradley. The place that emotion, as Mr. Lewis Freed says, occupies in Eliot's theory of poetry. is not due to scholasticism or to Kant but to Bradley.

Eliot says that poetry is the emotional equivalent of thought or recreation of thought into feeling. And he writes elsewhere that some lines of Donne's poems remain hovering between thought and feeling. These critical expressions of Eliot are not of course the paraphrasing of Bradley's philosophy or Bradley's theory of knowledge, but they are in the same vein. Eliot writes in his dissertation on Bradley : "There is no greater mistake than to think that feeling and thought are exclusive...."[46]

Thought and feeling are not mutually exclusive; they are one at bottom. Each participates, to a certain extent, in the other; and as it does, each is transformed and yet it does not altogether lose, its former character. For example, when thought is taken up into a whole of feeling (as in a poem), it is no longer thought, it ceases to be abstraction and takes on reality. Again when feeling is transformed into thought, it is no longer pure feeling, that is, no longer, as Bradley has it, "immediate". It has become an object of thought. Feeling can be felt, but can be known only by its objectification in thought, action and art. The difference between feeling and thought is that one is implicit and the other is explicit. That some lines of Donne, as pointed out by Eliot, hover between thought and feeling means that they have not been dragged into the light and made fully intelligible. In *Hamlet,* as Eliot points out, there has not been adequate objectification of feeling. The play hovers hardly beyond the periphery of feeling, and the feeling, though terrible, is without the correlation of object. Eliot wants that an artist in his art should deal, even with his own feelings and emotions, objectively and dispassionately. In his review titled — "*Ulysses*, Order and Myth", Eliot says that the artist should simply accept the material — material such as the feelings and emotions of his own life or the experiences of others. This material, as Eliot continues, is "not virtue to be enlarged or vice to be diminished". The emotions and the feelings of the writer himself are to be dealt within art like objective material. Eliot in his lecture "To Criticise the Critic" defines criticism in the terminology of F.H. Bradley as "the finding of bad reasons for what we believe upon instinct, but to find these reasons is no less an instinct."[47]

What rescued Eliot from the vortex of philosophy for poetry and literary criticism? A large part had been played by the influence, personal and immediate, of Ezra Pound. During the years 1915 to 1920 (when Pound left England) Eliot benefited, as he recalled in a contribution to *Purpose* in 1938, from Pound's "criticism of my poetry in our talk" and from — his indications of desirable territories to explore."

Pound had ready for Eliot the gallery of monitors. Active in his mind at the time were lessons which he had learned or elaborated, some in the company of Yeats, some in the company of Ford Madox Hueffer.

Ford's lesson was to say something naturally and briefly. He defined literary virtue as "the fewest possible words on your page". Pound picked up this lesson. Eliot appears to have accepted the advice, which agreed with his predisposition.

Pound influenced Eliot's poetry and criticism by his passion for economy, concreteness, and precision of expression. As is well known, Eliot's *The Waste Land* is dedicated to Ezra Pound. Pound's statement —"Go in fear of abstractions, that is, use concrete images having the hardness of cut-stone" — appealed immensely to the classical spirit of Eliot.

From Pound, Eliot inherited his translative method, his method of comparative study, and the concept of the scholar-critic. Eliot's call in one of his ealiest essays "Euripides and Professor Murray" for a timeless scholarship "which can assimilate both Homer and Flaubert" is almost a paraphrase of Pound's earlier demand for "a literary scholarship to weigh Theocritus and Mr. Yeats with one balance". Moreover, Eliot is indebted to Pound for a number of his specific doctrines — among them the concept of impersonalism and, according to Mario Praz, the doctrine of the "objective correlative". Eliot had a respect amounting to veneration for Pound, despite a basic religious disagreement and other quarrels, and regarded him as not only one of the greatest of contemporary critics but "probably the most important living poet in our language".

Pound's idea of poetry in *The Spirit of Romance* (1910 : page 5) as "a sort of inspired mathematics, which gives us equations not for abstract figure, triangles, spheres and the like, but equations for the human emotions" may be said to be the starting point of Eliot's theory of the objective correlative.[48] Pound's statements are not as clear-cut as Eliot's. The objective correlative can be really defined in Pound's terminology as mediation or equations for human emotions. The poem should be concrete in reference, objectifying a certain complex of feelings, finding the image, the set of symbols, the rhythmic design that will stir in the reader the emotions proper to the situations. When Pound speaks of an absolute rhythm or metaphor, he means a rhythm or metaphor completely appropriate to a feeling or emotion. The metaphor and rhythms are objective and the aim of the artist is to create objects, independent of his personal experience, that exactly correlates with a particular feeling or emotion. Hence, Eliot's "objective correlative". The poet is expressing not himself, but feelings and emotions that may or may not have correlation with his own feelings and emotions. The poet is not an agent or "medium" and it is not his business to make systems but, in Pound's terminology, "images" or "ideograms" and, in Eliot's, "objective correlative". Pound's insistence on the autonomy of the object, the concreteness of its presentation, the dramatic use of the persona or mask, points to the means of distancing oneself from the material while composing art — and this deeply appealed to Eliot.

Ezra Pound's most influential criticism is occasional. It has often taken the form of practical advice to other writers; Pound has not aspired to system-building. Pound's special critical emphasis reveals itself in a letter that he wrote in 1915 to Harriet Monroe : "Poetry," he says, "must be as well written as prose", a sentiment to be found in Eliot's Introduction to Samuel Johnson's "The Vanity of Human Wishes". In the same letter, Pound went on to clarify the prose-virtues that he had in mind :

> There must be no book-words, no periphrase, no inversions. It must be as simple as Maupassant's best prose, and as hard as Stendhal's....Rhythm must have meaning. It cannot be merely a careless dash off, with no grip and no real hold to the words and sense....

There must be no clichés, set phrases, stereotyped journalese. The only escape from such is by precision, a result of concentrated attention to what [one] is writing....objectivity and again objectivity, and expression : no hindside-beforeness, no straddled adjectives [as "addled mosses dank"] noTennysonianness of speech, nothing -nothing that you could not, in some circumstance, in stress of some emotion actually say.[49]

And what Pound says of "ideographic process" has some kinsship with Eliot's objective correlative. "[The ideographic] process is metaphor, the use of material images to suggest immaterial relations."[50]

The "ideographic" is an arrangement of concrete particulars ; there is a confrontation of these, yielding not a denatured abstraction, but a precise concrete experience. In constructing his ideograph, the poet is as impersonal as the scientist. Pound wrote in 1910 that poetry is a sort of finspired mathematics which gives equations not for abstract figures but for human emotions. Arthur Symons revealed Laforgue to Eliot, and Ezra Pound through his book *The Spirit of Romance* and still more through his table talk made Eliot aware of the greatness of Dante.

Eliot seems to be, as if, "ex-Pounding" the critical ideas on Dante, in his early essays in *The Sacred Wood* (1920), in his lecture on "Shakespeare and the Stoicism of Seneca" and his "Dante" of 1929. There is much resemblance between *The Spirit of Romance* of Pound and Eliot's statements on Dante. Pound makes dramatically a solemn vow to speak only with first-hand acquaintance of the text. More plainly he declares :

Throughout the book all critical statements are based on direct study of the texts themselves and not upon commentaries....After a few hours with the original, criticism becomes a vain thing.

Eliot's advice is to the same effect, though couched in a more guarded manner :

Read in this way it [the *Vita Nuoval]* can be more useful than a dozen commentaries [on the *Comedy*].

In either case, the author emphasises the fact that he is a

poet, and commentaries are apt to obscure one's appreciation. Pound writes an important point about allegory :

> We get the Allegory, a sort of extension of the fable....In romances he [the medieval author] has hold of actions and speech and has generalised about emotions. In the allegory he learns to separate himself, not from complete moods, but from simple qualities and passions, and to visualise them.[51]

Another passage of Pound illustrates for the *Commedia* the point of view which is virtually the theory of "objective correlative" :

> There is little doubt that Dante conceived the real Hell, Purgatory, and Paradise as states, and not places....For the purpose of art and popular religion it is more convenient to deal with such matters objectively....It is therfore expedient in reading the *Commedia* to regard Dante's descriptions of the actions and conditions of thades as descriptions of men's mental states in life, in which they are, after death, compelled to continue : that is to say, man's inner selves stand visibly before the eyes of Dante's intellect.[52]

The points made by Pound in *The Spirit of Romance* are : allegory is a means for the poet to separate himself from the emotions, to visualise them; this kind of vision is not a pretence, there is nothing rhetorical about it; the attempt of the poet to reproduce exactly the thing he has actually seen, makes for clarity.

If now we read what Eliot says on the same subject in his essay on Dante, we will easily perceive the affinities. The allegorical method, to Eliot, makes for simplicity and intelligibility and Eliot says that allegory means clear visual images. In Pound's definition of allegory as a method "to separate oneself from emotions", one finds the germ, and a clear glimpse, of Eliot's objective correlative.

One can add in Pound's vein that for Eliot the objective correlative is a more convenient method to deal with emotional experience objectively and through the objective correlative the poet's "inner selves" or emotions stand visibly before the eyes of the reader.

Pound's influence is closely connected with Eliot's

interpretation of Dante's allegory which is in terms of "clear visual images, a concise and luminous language".

"Clear visual images" and "a concise luminous language" are the two qualities of Dante which Eliot has in mind. The former, as Mario Praz says, is the objective correlative of the emotions they intend to suggest and the latter appeals to the auditory imagination.

Eliot's theory of impersonality can also be traced back to his reading of Professor Grand Gent's *Dante* (New York, 1916), a book to which Eliot gives the first place in the list of works that have influenced him. Professor Gent writes :

> In no respect, perhaps, do medieval writings differ more patently from modern than in their dignified impersonality. Contrast this attitude for a moment with our presentday effusiveness, our pitiful eagerness to disclose to any one who will listen, each petty detail of our bodily and spiritual existence....Such a display would once have seemed almost as indecent as walking naked in the street....

We thus, see how some of the most characteristic utterances of Eliot about the theory of the objective correlative and of the impersonality of the poet grew in connection with his study of Dante.

Through Pound and through the pages of the *Egoist,* Eliot became aware of Joyce. In the *Egoist,* where in 1917 he replaced Aldington as Assistant Editor, he saw the first chapter of *Ulysses.* The early chapter of *Ulysses* seen at the *Egoist* office and later chapters which Joyce sent for his opinion, Eliot read as poems. He told Joyce certain chapters were "superb" and "I have nothing but admiration; in fact, I wish, for my own sake, that I had not read it."

Eliot reviewed *Ulysses* in the *Dial* of November 1923 and claimed that Joyce had invented a new use of "myth" which was diffused throughout his novel by the manipulation of "a continuous parallel between centemporaneity and antiquity" ; the technique had "the importance of a scientific discovery", and others would adopt it in their independent ways.

In October 1922 Eliot launched *The Criterion* as a quarterly which lasted till 1939.

Another literary figure and eminent thinker who exercised considerable influence on Eliot's work and personality, was T.E. Hulme. Though Eliot never met him, on reaching London he found that the literary atmosphere was surcharged with the impact Hulme had left on a circle of brilliant writers and philosophers. Hulme was a firm believer in the philosophy of Original Sin and the inability of man to be perfect. Speaking of Hulme in *The Criterion* in 1924, Eliot qualified him as "the forerunner of a new attitude of mind which should be the twentieth century mind, if the twentieth century is to have a mind of its own." "Hulme," he said, "is classical, reactionary and revolutionary; he is the antipodes of the eclectic, tolerant and democratic mind of the end of the last century."

Eliot was strongly influenced by T.E. Hulme's antiliberal-humanist tradition. Hulme's belief in Original Sin stirred, as it were, a similar belief and impression in Eliot. The Georgian tradition was leading English poetry to looseness. vagueness and sloppiness, and Eliot found in Hulme's attitude to life and art almost a weapon to expose the obscurantism. and charlatanism prevailing in the poetry of his time. Hulme has been important and radical for Eliot not only for his belief in Original Sin and the imperfection of man but also for his cult of dry, hard, classical, concrete art. Herbert Read while introducing *Speculations* wrote that Hulme was the foe of obscurantism, and Jacob Epstein in his Foreword to the same book said about Hulme that he was a terror to "fumistes" and charlatans of all kinds. The greater part of the Renaissance, of Rousseauism and of ninteenth century Romanticism centres round the emotional and vague idealisation of man and his perfection. As a result, the extension and the aggrandisement of personality had become a cult with the Romantic poets of the nineteenth century. Poetry had taken an unhealthy turn under the cloak of esotericism and ambiguity or it was simply what Eliot calls in a different context "popping over with sentiment". In England in the nineteenth century a poet generally did not regard a poem as poem unless it was 'moaning" or "whining".

Eliot fully agrees with the T.E. Hulme of *Speculations*. Hulme's absolute differentiation between Humanism and the religious attitude draws the full assent of Eliot. Eliot like Hulme does not believe in the principle of "continuity". Eliot is quite similar to Hulme in the opinion that "the divine" is not life at its intensest. This is manifest in Eliot's essay on Babbitt.

Hulme in *Speculations* says that the "discontinuities" are not only apparent but real and he thinks it necessary to realise that there is an absolute and not a relative difference between humanism and the religious spirit. Hulme is disgusted with the trivial and the accidental characteristics of living shapes and searches for an austerity, a monumental stability and permanence, a perfection and rigidity which vital things can never have. And this leads to the use of forms which can almost be called "geometrical". Romanticism, Hulme says, confuses the human and the divine, and never separates them. The main reproachable point about it is that it blurs the clear outlines of human relations — in political thought or in the literary treatment of sex — by introducing in them the perfection that properly belongs to the non-human. It is fallacious to think that one will move to progress after the abolition of discipline and restriction. Hulme intensifies, to some extent, the art of rigour, classicism, discipline, system and restriction and the belief in the supernatural in T.S. Eliot. This is confirmed also by the fact Eliot, in his essays on Pascal and Baudelaire, refers approvingly to Hulme. Eliot quotes Hulme's lines in his essay on Baudelaire :

> In the light of these absolute values, man himself is judged to be essentially limited and imperfect. He is endowed with Original Sin. While he can occasionally accomplish acts which partake of perfection, he can never himself be perfect. Certain secondary results in regard to ordinary human action in society follow from this. A man is essentially bad, he can only accomplish anything of value by discipline — ethical and political. Order is not merely negative, but creative and liberating. Institutions are necessary.[53]

Hulme's sense of tradition and organisation has strengthened a similar sense in Eliot. From the angle of authority, tradition, institution, some form of discipline — religious or supernatural

— Eliot examines many issues and authors. He says that Blake's poetry has the unpleasantness and honesty of a great writer but Blake's naked vision and powerful imagination are in need of being guided and restrained by some sense of external authority or institution. Eliot makes an almost similar point when he says Hardy has in his work the expression of his personality wholly uncurbed by any institutional attachment or submission to any objective beliefs. D.H. Lawrence too, in Eliot's opinion, lacks in social training and tradition. Eliot says that Lawrence's ordinary insensibility to morality is a "monstrosity".

Hulme writes that a classical revival is coming, and for it "fancy" will be superior to imagination. Eliot defends fancy and criticises Coleridge's ideas on Imagination, saying that it is wrong to have poor associations about fancy, as Coleridge does.

Hulme objects to the sloppiness of the Romantics. A pseudo-Romanticist does not consider a poem as a poem unless it is 'moaning" or "whining" about something or other. He adds that a poem which is all hard, a properly classical poem, would not be considered poetry at all. They say poetry is not poetry, unless it is damp.

In many places in his critical essays Eliot defends accuracy, definiteness of description and expression, beauty of structure, shapeliness and design, simplicity and clarity in poetry. Eliot does not suppose that a poem will not be a poem unless it has "rnagic casements". Even a "minor" poem, according to Eliot, is not necessarily without significance. It has probably the first requisite of poetry, in the sense that it is competent and correct. It is not all the time poetry but *verse*, and it is lucid, definite, accurate, precise, legitimate.

Two important events helped to precipitate Eliot's idea of impersonality. One was the publication by the Egoist Press in 1917 of A *Portrait of the Artist as a Young Man*. The other was the intensive propaganda campaign which Pound conducted on behalf of Rémy de Gourmont's criticism between 1917 and 1920.

David E. Ward points out that one of dé Gourmont's constant themes is the relationship between the man as artist and the man in actual life, the relationship between the style and the man, and between the work of art and the artist.

The influence of Rémy de Gourmont on Eliot is clear from the fact that Eliot has quoted a significant passage from Rémy de Gourmont's *Le Problem du style* in his essay on Massinger :

> Flaubert incorporait toute sa sensibilité à ses oeuvres....Hors de ses liveres, oij il se transvasait goutte à goutte, jusqu'à la lie, Flaubert est fort peu intéressant.[54]

The fundamental point that Rémy de Gourmont wants to highlight is of infusing personality into a work of art almost "goutte A goutte" (*i.e.*, drop by drop). He says that the work of Flaubert which has this infusion of personality almost "drop by drop" is important and significant. One of Eliot's favourite quotations from Rémy de Gourmont is that the critic's task is "eriger en lois ses impréssions personnelles" ("the erection of impressions into laws").

In 1925 Eliot discussed Arnold in *The Criterion,* suggesting that Arnold was "no critic", but some of his prose was "a perpetual inspiration." Eliot sees much in Arnold that he does not like. But the basic similarity of intentions exists. To see the object as it really is and disinterestedness, are the Arnoldian recipes. This kind of insistence is found in Eliot also. "They know the whole, we know the parts" was Arnold's diagnosis of the malady, and Eliot says in a similar vein that we have to see life steadily and see it whole. Eliot's "Tradition and the Individual Talent" is in the best sense in the Arnoldian vein.

Both critics are classicists biased towards tradition and authority. If Arnold has semi-ethical criteria, Eliot also, after his conversion, in some essays, specially "Religion and Literature", advocates religious and ethical principles in literature.

Eliot had a high opinion as well as a fascination for Henry James. Eliot includes Henry James among his masters. Sometimes he mentions his name in parallel construction with Dante and Shakespeare. The word "Pattern" given currency by Henry James became the forte of Eliot as poet and critic. Eliot writes while introducing Professor Wilson Knight's *The Wheel of Fire* that great novelists and the great poets in their works of art have a pattern. Pattern denotes consistency and a point of view, and so meaning emerges from the whole work. Eliot says what is important in poetry is not feeling but the pattern of feeling that it makes. Eliot

examines John Ford from this viewpoint of pattern and finds that
Ford's work has none of the internal organs of poetry and no
pattern. Alan Holder in his article "Eliot on Henry James" has
conjecture about the actual or principal source of the catalyst
metaphor. He writes that Eliot might have drawn upon one of
James's prefaces which says that the novelist's use of actual
persons should be thought of

> in chemical....terms. We can surely account for nothing,
> in the noveliest's work that has not passed through the
> crucible of his imagination, has not, in that perpetually
> simmering cauldron, his intellectual pot-au-feu, been
> reduced to savoury fusion. We have to figure the
> morsel, of course, not as boiled to nothing, but as
> exposed, in return for the taste it gives out, to a new
> and richer saturation. It has entered....into new relations,
> it emerges for new ones. Its final savour has been
> constituted, but its prime identity destroyed.[55]

A remark in one of Keats's Letters is cited by Eliot with
great admiration and this seems to be the main source of the
catalyst metaphor of Eliot. Keats writes :

> Men of Genius are great as certain ethereal chemicals
> operating on the mass of neutral intellect but they have
> not any individuality, any determined character.[56]

Washington Alston's *Lectures on Art is* held to be the real
source of the phrase "objective correlative". Washington Alston,
the American painter and critic, wrote :

> So too, is the external world to the mind ; which needs,
> also as the condition of its manifestation, its objective
> correlative. Hence, the pressure of some outward
> object.[57]

Despite their basic Opposition of views, I.A. Richards has
been one of the major influences on Eliot's critical thought. Eliot
has often dwelt upon his indebtedness to Richards and has found
his work "of cardinal importance in the history of literary
criticism." Eliot has certainly taken from the early Richards one
of the basic concepts, the theory of irrelevancy of belief to poetic
appreciation, both in the reader and (with reservations) in the
poet. Eliot has resisted Richards' basic scientific orientation,

frequently with sharp attack but at the same time borrowing many of its concepts and a good deal of its vocabulary.

John M. Steadman in *Notes and Queries*[58] says that in actuality there are reasonable grounds for regarding Eliot's "objective correlative" as an unconscious borrowing from Edmund Husserl (Edmund Husserl's *Logische unter suchungen,* third edition), As early as 1900 and 1901 Edmund Husserl had employed the terms "gagenstand liches Korrelate" and "objectives Korrelate" in *Logische unter suchungen.* Distinguishing sharply between categories of meaning on the one hand and the objective categories on the other, he regarded the latter as "Objective correlatives" of the former.

John M. Steadman writes further that Eliot's phrase derives either from Husserl's own writings or else from some secondary discussion of phenomenology — which seems, on the whole, extremely probable. Eliot is however apparently the first to transfer it from logical theory to literary criticism. T.E. Hulme also had shown an interest in Husserl's phenomenology *(Speculations, 1942,* pp. 18, 28, 39, 62-3, 257).

Steadman adds that Eliot's indebtedness to Husserl moreover appears to have been essentially verbal rather than conceptual. His "objective" and Husserl's "objective Korrelate" denote altogether different concepts. In adopting the term to his poetic theory, he divested it of its original meaning.

Pater is negatively the source of Eliot's objective correlative.[59] Eliot's essay on *Hamlet* is curiously preoccupied with Pater. Eliot remarks :

> Probably more people have thought *Hamlet* a work of art because they found it interesting, than have found it interesting because it is a work of art. It is the Mona Lisa of literature.

The reference here seems, at least in part, to be to the notorious passage in Pater's essay "Leonardo da Vinci", first published in 1869 and included in *Studies in the History of the Renaissance* (1873). We cannot be quite certain that it is the Leonardo essay that Eliot has in mind, but the passage is certainly one of the best known in the history of nineteenth century criticism, and of course Eliot knew Pater's *Renaissance* well. But the clearest evidence of Eliot's intention is his long consideration of Pater, "Arnold and Pater" (1930), in which he accuses Pater of bring incapable of "seeing any work of art simply as it is", spacially because of his inclination "to emphasise whatever is morbid or associated with physical malady". Eliot says that this becomes, in Paters essay on Leonardo and Giorgione, "a preoccupation, coming between him and the object as it really is."[60]

In "Sandro Botticelli", included in the *Renaissance*, Pater has given several hints which suggest a source for the criterion of the "Objective Correlative" and consequently explain Pater's otherwise apparently uncalled-for presence in Eliot's essay on *Hamlet*.

Pater is concerned with defining the way in which Botticelli went beyond "the simple religion and the simple naturalism of his predecessors". He painted them [religious incidents] with an undercurrent of original sentiment, which touches one as the real matter of the picture through the veil of its ostensible subject. Pater develops later the subjectivity, the lack of equivalence between the outward data and the personal mood that they invoke which he sees as "the peculiar quality of pleasure" that we find uniquely in Botticelli's work :

> But the genius of which Botticelli is the type usurps the data before it as the exponent of ideas, moods visions of its own; in this interest, it plays fast and loose with those data....[61]

Significantly the valuations are diametrically opposed for Eliot. *Hamlet* is "most" certainly "an artistic failure", because of the lack of "adequacy of the external to the emotion"; for Pater, Botticelli is an "entire" artist who suggests the true complexion of humanity precisely because he suggests an "original sentiment", a "peculiar sensation" not immediately evoked by the external facts.

Pater's appreciative description of Botticelli provides Eliot an ideal example of objectionable imprecision and subjectivity, suggestive of Romantic art. By reversing the judgment of success but retaining the same elements in the artistic equation, Eliot applies to *Hamlet* a new criterion of "adequacy", condemns the Romantic, pathological art of the play, and in so doing establishes, at least in theory and for his own purposes, an objective, anti-Romantic theory of drama and poetry.

According to Eliot, Oscar Wilde is a "most vocal" aesthete and not a "most professional" one. But many of Oscar Wilde's thoughts have influenced Eliot's thoughts as well, though he has carefully avoided any reference to Wilde. We cannot say that Eliot did not study Oscar Wilde's works. The personal life of Oscar Wilde might have repulsed Eliot. Hence, Eliot is reticent about his debt to Wilde. Eliot says that it is not the particular emotions or experiences of a writer that count but the artistic process, the pressure under which the fusion of "floating emotions" takes place. Impressions important for a man may play quite a negligible part or may have no place in his poetry, and those important in poetry may play quite a negligible part in the man.

The same idea may be found in Oscar Wilde when he discusses art and its relation to nature :

> The public imagine that because they are interested in their immediate surroundings, Art also should be in them, and should take them as her subject-matter. But the mere fact that they are interested in these things makes them unsuitable subject for Art....To Art's subject-matter we should be more or less indifferent. We should at any rate, have no preference, no prejudices, no partition-feeling of any kind.[62]

As examples, Eliot mentions, among others, the murder of Agamemnon which has been animated by the art of a poet who is standing aloof from the event. Oscar Wilde also affirmed the ancient distinction between truth and poetic truth : "....There was hardly one of the dramatists who did not recognise that the object of Art is not simple truth but complex beauty."

According to Eliot the stream of tradition is to be studied by the artist, and it is interesting to find a version of this in Oscar Wilde's *Intentions* : "But there has never been creative age that has not been critical also."[63] And more :

Earnest : For the creative faculty is higher than the critical, there is really no comparison between them.

58   THE DYNAMICS OF CRITICISM IN T.S. ELIOT

Gilbert : The antithesis between them is entirely arbitrary. Without the critical faculty, there is no artistic creation at all worthy of the name.[64]

Eliot's auditory imagination stresses the feeling for the rhythmic quality of language. Of Arnold Eliot says : "I am not sure that Arnold was sensitive to the musical qualities....what I call the auditory imagination penetrating far below the conscious levels....sinking to the primitive and forgotten." Wilde has similarly observed in a less pontifical vein : "Music always seems to me to produce that effect. It creates for one a past of which one has been ignorant, and fills one with a sense of sorrows that have been hidden from one's tears."[65]

REFERENCES

1. "American Literature and Language", *To Criticise the Critic,* pp. 43-44.
2. *Ibid.,* p. 45.
3. *The Times Literary Supplement,* 14, March 1929.
4. Herbert Howarth : *Notes on Some Figures behind T.S. Eliot,* p. 66 (Chatto & Windus, 1965).
5. *Ibid.,* p. 68.
6. *Ibid.,* p. 74
7. "What Dante Means to Me", *To Criticise the Critic,* p. 125.
8. *A Garland for John Donne,* edited by Theodore Spencer, Gloucester, Mass., Peter Smith, 1958.
9. "The Critical Writings of George Santayana", *Scrutiny,* Vol. 4, 1935-36, p. 278.
10. G. Santayana, *Three Philosophical Poets* (Doubleday Anchor Books, 1953).
11. *Ibid.,* pp. 121-22.
12. *Interpretation of Poetry and Religion* (1918), pp. 263-64, 277 (Charles Scribner's Sons & Constable & Sons Ltd.).
13. *Scrutiny,* Vol. IV, 1935-36, p. 294.
14. *Athenaeum, 25,* April 1919, p. 236.
15. Herbert Howarth : *Notes on Some Figures behind T.S. Eliot,* p. 89.
16. *Ibid.,* p. 91
17. "Baudelaire and the Symbolists", reviewed by T.S. Eliot, *The Criterion,* Vol. IX (January 1930), pp. 357-59.
18. *Axel's Castle,* p. 82 (The Fontana Library, 1967).
19. "Kipling" : On *Poetry and Poets,* 1956, p. 238. "The Music of Poetry", *On Poetry and Poets,* p. 38.
21. *To Criticise the Critic,* p. 22.
22. *Ibid.,* p. 126.
23. *Selected Essays,* p. 422.
24. *Ibid.,* p. 434

25. *To Criticise the Critic, p.* 15.
26. *Notes on Some Figures behind T.S. Eliot, p.* 128.
27. *Ibid.*
28. *Ibid.,* p. 123.
29. *Selected Essays,* p. 476
30. *Ibid.,* p. 491.
31. Herbert Howarth : *Notes on Some Figures behind T.S. Eliot,* p. 152.
32. "Eliot and Bergson", *The Review of English Studies,* N.S., Vol. XVI, No. 70, May 1967, pp. 149-61, 174-76.
33. *The Use of Poetry,* p. 102.
34. *American Literature and Language* : St. Louis, 1953, p. 20.
35. "Experiment in Criticism" (1929) an Essay by Eliot; *Literary Opinion in America,* Vol. 2, edited by M.D. Zabel, Harper and Row Publishers, New York.
36. "Blake": *The Sacred Wood,* p.154 (Methuen & Co. Ltd., London, 7th Edition, 1950).
37. *Egoist,* 1918, pp. 69-70.
38. The Borderline of Prose", *New Statesman,* IX, 1919, p. 158.
39. Rhyme and Reason", *The Listener, 111,* 1930, p. 503.
40. Henri Bergson: *Time and Free Will,* p. 116.
41. Smidt Kristian : Poetry *and Belief in the Work of T.S. Eliot :* (1961), p. 163.
42. *To Criticise the Critic,* p. 17.
43. *Notes on Some Figures behind T.S. Eliot* (Chatto & Windus, 1965), p. 182.
44. *T.S. Eliot,* edited by Hugh Kenner, p. 41 (A Spectum Book, 1962).
45. Eliot's preface, *Knowledge and Experience,* p. 10 (Faber & Faber, 1965).
46. T.S. Eliot : *Knowledge and Experience,* p. 18.
47. *To Criticise the Critic* (1965), p. 21.
48. "Eliot and Dante" : The *Southern Review,* No. 4, pp. 525-48.
49. *Letters of Ezra Pound,* edited by D.D. Paige, New York, 1950, pp. 48-46.
50. *Instigations,* p. 376.
51. Ezra Pound : *The Spirit of Romance* (1910), p. 5.
52. Quoted by Mario Praz, *T.S. Eliot,* edited by Leonard Unger, p. 301 (Rinehart & Company).
53. *Selected Essays,* p. 430.
54. *Ibid.*
55. Quoted by Alan Holder, "Eliot on Henry Jamas", *PMLA,* 1964, September, p. 490.
56. *The Use of Poetry,* p. 101.
57. Washington Alston's *Lectures on Art* (1850), edited by H.H. Dana, p. 16.
58. *Notes and Queries,* June, 1958, Vol, 203, p. 261.
59. "Pater and Eliot" : *Modern Language Quarterly, Vol.* 26, 1965, p. 426.
60. *Selected Essays,* pp. 439-40.
61. Walter Pater : *The Renaissance,* pp. 53-54 (Ist Edition).
62. *Intentions,* p. 116.
63. *Ibid.*
64. *Ibid.*
65. *Ibid.*

3
The Aesthetic of Verse

In this chapter, I have attempted an extended, critical consideration of the principles, formulations and definitions of poetry given by Eliot at different places and on different occasions. Eliot has not written his critical essays under any systematic plan; his books are collections of reviews, introductions and addresses; yet coherently progressing principles of poetry do emerge from them.

Among the aesthetic principles of Eliot, the aesthetic of verse is of paramount importance. Eliot writes that his essays and formulations about poetry are the by-product of his poetry-workshop or the prolongation of his thinking on the composition of his own poems, yet one feels that Eliot's writing or talking about poetry is in no way less absorbing than his poetry itself. In his respect, the case of Paul Valéry is somewhat similar to that Eliot. It is probable that Eliot's poetry, through the passage of time, may go out of fashion, but his formulations and explanations of poetry will provide a permanent fund of critical stimulus to the reader.

It is part of the modesty of Eliot to say that he is no aesthetician. The fact is that whenever Eliot dwells upon poetry he brings adequate illumination on the problems and the essence of poetry. Regarding the definition or the critical appraisal of poetry, Eliot is a specialist. It is very difficult to be wholly new in defining poetry, because poetry is as mysterious as the very soul of man. Eliot apparently seems to us revolutionary; yet in fact, what he has done as poet and critic, is that he has given new emphases. It is proof of great courage that Eliot introduced a new turn and new points of emphasis regarding the precept and practice of poetry, when poetry was almost famishing and literary criticism becoming sickly through excessive romanticism. Eliot realised that the traditional nineteenth century way of writing poetry was incapable of registering the urban squalor, the seediness and the dinginess of the twentieth century-life. Sentimentalizing over a daisy or a daffodil could no more be continued in a grim urban environment.

In his essay "Tradition and the Individual Talent" (1919), Eliot gave an important definition of poetry which, though wellknown, deserves to be quoted : "Poetry is not a turning loose of emotion, but an escape from emotion ; it is not the expression of personality, but an escape from personality."[1]

In this definition, a new emphasis is manifest. Eliot at the most opportune moment demanded a check over the increasing sentimentalization of poetry. The uncritical or the hasty reader may get a wrong impression from this definition. It is just possible that he may conclude that Eliot is in favour of dry, dull or only classical poetry, or such poetry as has no room for emotion and passion. While reading the earlier essays and definitions of poetry, one must have in one's mind the background and the context in which they were written. Eliot himself writes : "I was in reaction, not only against Georgian poetry, but against Georgian criticism; I was writing in a context which the reader of today has either forgotten or has never experienced."[2]

Vagueness, emotionalism and pseudo-Romanticism had become the order of the day. Eliot aimed to bring a healh balance and order, a clarity and sanity in poetry. In the expression : "Poetry is not a turning loose of emotion....but an escape from personality," "Turning loose of emotion" denotes, indirectly or implicitly, the worse features of the nineteenth century Romanticism. In the eighteen-eighties, the typical reader of poetry was content to tolerate looseness, vagueness and emotionalism, at the cost of the other qualities of poetry. Eliot determined to give a jolt to the Georgian sensibility. "Turning loose of emotion" is an expression, metaphorical enough, which, adequately and sharply, suggests that excessive, haphazard, indefinite, messy, sloppy and misty jumbles of emotion will not make good poetry or good art. And "escape from emotion" appears to us extreme and somewhat exaggerated, as no real poetry is possible if it involves complete detachment from emotion. Specially in the earlier essays, Eliot takes an exaggeratedly opposite course from the usual one of the Georgian period, simply because he reacts against it and has to establish in the reader's mind some other values and traits of poetry which have been neglected for a long time. The study of Arthur Symons' *The Symbolist Movement in Literature* forced upon Eliot's mind a realisation that a new kind of verse was needed in order to picture and render the city-life of skyscrapers, madding crowds, industrialisation, the combustion engine, slums and jazzy machines. While introducing a dramatic poem *(Savonarola)* by his mother, Eliot made a point of much significance : "Perhaps the conditions of modern life (think how large a part is now played in our sensory life by the internal combustion engine) have altered our rhythms.[3]

Eliot's definiton of poetry as an escape from "emotion" and "personality" is not, as a partial reader may hastily conclude, exactly antithetical to Wordsworth's definition "Poetry is the spontaneous overflow of powerful feeling it takes its origin from emotions recollected in tranquillity." Here the difference lies in the fact that Eliot insists, more outspokenly, on disciplining and calming the "overflow" of powerful feelings in good poetry. In a radio talk,[4] Eliot expressed his unstinted liking for Wordsworth's poem, "Resolution and Independence."

The nineteenth century poets and critics harped mostly on emotion and sensation, and Eliot in reaction laid excessive stress on wit, intelligence, levity and commonsense, structure and organisation in poetry. Eliot writes relevantly.

> There are many people who appreciate the expression
> of sincere emotion in verse and there is a small —
> number of people who can appreciate technical
> excellence.[5]

Matthew Arnold, in his essay on Gray, writes slightingly of eighteenth century poetry. Eliot tries to assert that the poetry of Pope or Dryden or Johnson is not necessarily inferior; rather, some of its qualities hold good for the poetry of any age. Literary finish, purity of language and clarity are prose virtues which should not be bypassed. Such prose virtues are the permanent ingredients of poetry. Arnold says :

The difference between genuine poetry and the poelry
of Dryden, Pope and all their school, is briefly this :
their poetry is conceived and composed in their wits,
genuine poetry is conceived and composed in the Soul.[6]

Apparently, "soul", for Arnold, symbolises emotion, passion,
sensation or feeling in the typical Romantic way. Arnold's
definition, in fact, is not wholly incorrect, but it seems to overlook
other qualities and faculties of man, like wit, reasoning and
ratiocinative power. It is narrowness on Arnold's part to use wit
in this limited sense. Eliot has rightly pointed out, in his essay on
Marvell, that the Oxford Dictionary warrants us against using the
word "wit" in the superficial sense. Unlike Arnold, Eliot takes
"wit" in the larger sense, and deplores in general its absence in
poetry. His discussion of poetry and its problems is done with
cool-headedness, commonsense, and a sense of proportion. Arnold's
statement — "genuine poetry is conceived and composed in the
soul" — means virtually a directive for the poet "to look into
your heart and write."[7] Eliot says convincingly and interestingly
that a poet should look into a good deal more than the heart; the
good poet must look into the cerebral cortex, the nervous system
and the digestive tracts. Eliot means to say that good poetry is
not merely sensation but also cerebration, not only passion but
also ratiocination. Eliot is appreciative of the best of the seventeenth
century metaphysical poetry because it makes varied recalcitrant
qualities operate in harmony and union.

Regarding emotion in poetry, Eliot believes that it should not
be loose, indefinite and excessive, for sentimentalization makes for
bad art. Shakespeare is the greater artist by virtue of his power to
scale down and control the mounting squads of emotion in *King
Lear* through the Fool's laughter. "A slumber did my spirit seal"
presents the same kind of control over a powerful emotion;
underneath, there is the surge and swirl of the tragic experience,
but the surface is calm.

Eliot differentiates between the art-emotion and the crude
emotion of man outside art. He calls the art-emotion the aesthetic
one, and explains further that emotion in good art is complex,
richer and more definite than any emotion of human life. The
emotional experiences of people in general are overflowing,

diffuse, indefinite, floating, opaque and abstract. Emotion in good poetry has force, particularity, relevance and concreteness, Eliot writes :

> His [a poet's] particular emotion may be simple or crude or flat. The emotion in his poetry will be a complex thing, but not with the complexity of the emotion of people who have very complex or unusual emotions in life.[8]

And at another place :

> The effect of a work of art upon the person who enjoys it is an experience different in kind from any experience not of art.[9]

But I.A. Richards in his essay "The Phantom Aesthetic State" is vehemently critical of the so-called, "aeshetic experience" and its differentiation from other kinds of experience of life. This kind of differentiation between art-emotion and non-art-emotion in Eliot's manner arouses I.A. Richards' remark, "the phantom problem of the aesthetic mode or aesthetic state, a legacy from the days of abstract investigations...."[10] I.A. Richards says :

> When we look at a picture, or read a poem or listen to music, we are not doing something quite unlike what we were doing on our way to the gallery or when we dressed in the morning. The fashion in which the experience is caused in us, is different, and as a rule, the experience is more complex. and, if we are successful, more unified. But our activity is not of a fundamentally different kind.[11]

That emotion in art, according to Eliot, is definite, means that it is fully objectified and is truly relevant to a particular object and situation. Good art has usually definite emotion, and Eliot highly commends it anywhere he finds it. In his review, "The Silurist", Eliot shows the superiority of George Herbert's poetry over the poetry of Henry Vaughan. "In short the emotion of Herbert is clear, definite, mature and sustained, whereas, the emotion of Vaughan is vague, adolescent, fitful and retrogressive.[12]

About this point, Eliot writes in another place :

> ....he [Swinburne] uses the most general word, because his emotion is never particular, never in direct line of vision, never focused; when you take to pieces any

verse of Swinburne, yoit find always that the object was not there...only the word.[13]

Thus, the indefinite emotion in absence of the definite object is abstract and nebulous. Without the definite object and emotion a poem will be wanting in "relevant intensity." The following lines of Ezra Pound might have influenced T.S. Eliot :

....The only kind of emotion worthy of a poet is the inspirational emotion which energizes and strengthens, and which is remote from the everyday emotion of sloppiness and sentiment....Go in fear of abstraction....consider the definiteness of Dante's presentation as compared with Milton's....[14]

Eliot showers high praise on definite emotion and takes it as a sign of good poetry. He writes :

Instead of slightly veiled and resonant abstractions, like [those] of Swinburne, or the mossiness of Mallarme, Pound's verse has always definite emotion behind it.[15]

Though *Speculations* was published in 1924, Eliot's attitude to poetry is very similar to that of T.E. Hulme. David Daiches writes lucidly about Hulme :

For Hulme there is classicism (good) and romanticism (bad); abstract or geometrical art (good) and naturalistic (bad); the religious attitude (good) and humanism (bad); belief in original sin (good) and confidence in man (bad); hard, clear, precise images (good) and imagination (bad); discipline (good) and self-expression (bad); dictatorship or at least royalism (good) and democracy (bad).[16]

Hulme is inclined to shift the interest from the content to the medium, or from the sincerity of experience to the making and shaping of a poem.

Eliot's attitude is no less extreme. The composition of a poem is to him almost like the making of a leg of a table, or a jug or an engine. Hulme in his *Speculations* writes that the new art is geometrical in character while the art we are accustomed to, is vital. The geometrical art, he continues, most obviously exhibits no delight in nature and no striving after vitality. Its forms are always what can be described as stiff and lifeless. The geometrical art is something absolutely distinct and free from the messiness, the confusion and the accidental details of existing things. Hulme says further : "As far as sensibility goes, you get a kind of shrinking from anything that has the appearance of being mechanical."[17]

Eliot's reaction against the nineteenth century attitude to poetry is similar to T.E. Hulme's : "For it is not the greatness or the intensity of the emotion, the components, but the intensity of the artistic process, the pressure so to speak, under which the fusion takes place, that counts."

Though Eliot has used the term "objective correlative" concerning *Hamlet, it* is valid for almost every form of art. The "objective correlative" guarantees the definiteness, balance and relevance of the poem. The lack of it is likely to turn the emotion ineffectual and confused. That good poetry does usually have an "objective correlative" means that the feelings and emotions in it are not without an object or beyond the context of facts and events — imagined or real. That is the universal formula which is true for the best poetry of any age. In a poem, emotion accompanied by an object, and attached to a particular situation has tremendous particularity and force.

Eliot like Hulme leans on the side of classicism and has a general predisposition towards order and discipline. His chief concern is that feeling and emotion should not become unmanageable in art. He wants the artist to treat feelings and emotions — emotions bearing even upon his own person — as something objective. Eliot writes significantly, in this context, in a review, *"Ulysses,* Order and Myth."[18] that in creation one is responsible for what one can do with the material, which one must simply accept. Eliot includes, in this material, the emotions and feelings of the writer himself, which for the writer are simply material — which he must accept — and are not "virtues to be enlarged or vices to be diminished". Eliot in his book *Knowledge and Experience* attempts to present feelings as something objective. He writes :

....Our ordinary speech declares that two people may share the same feeling as well as regard the same object yet we persist in believing that about feelings there is something private, that we cannot know them from the outside; although we are compelled to admit that often an observer understands a feeling better than does the person who experiences it....feelings exist on the same footing as other object : they are equally public....[19]

It is obvious that we can no more explain passion to a person who has never experienced it than we can explain light to the blind. But it should be obvious also that we can explain the passion equally well : it is no more subjective because some persons have never experienced it, than light is subjective because the blind cannot see. We can explain it by its relations; by its eflects upon the heart-beat, its toxic alterations of the system, by its effects in the conduct of social intercourse....[20]

Eliot does not always treat emotion and feeling in one sense; he takes emotion to be part of feeling, as the canvas of the latter is greater than that of the former. Emotion is generally taken to be distinct and definite, whereas feeling is regarded as a little obscure, more tangled, faint and less violent. The function of the artist is to make the configuration of feelings into a definite set or pattern. Eliot says that there may be vague thought but precise feeling. And precise feelings take the shape of definite emotions. Introducing The *Art of Poetry* by Paul Valéry, Eliot writes that poetry is important not for the feelings but for the pattern of feelings that it makes.

Eliot sometimes uses "feeling" as shorter units which the artist or the poet coheres and systematises into one definite emotional structure. And sometimes he uses feelings for experiences which are not usually regarded as fit subject-matter for poetry : "The business of the poet....is to express feelings which are not in actual emotions at all."[21]

Eliot's differentiation of feeling from emotion is not quite clear; yet it is a markedly valuable contribution to aesthetic principles. Feelings are considered by Eliot as various indefinite experiences which are compounded into a harmonious whole by the artist in art :

> The poet's mind is, in fact, a receptacle for seizing and storing up numberless feelings, phrases, images which remain there until all the particles which can unite to form a new compound are present together.[22]

....Great poetry may be made without the direct use of any emotion whatever : composed out of feelings solely.[23]

In "Tradition and the Individual Talent" Eliot defines poetry negatively only to assert his viewpoint more positively. Eliot has dwelt upon the formulation and explanation of poetry in a debator's style, with a new emphasis and powerful rhetoric — sharp-edged, hard-hitting, deliberately partial, almost dogmatic.

Poetry, Eliot says, is not the expression of personality but an escape from personality. Eliot does not like to be drawn into any clear-cut discussion of personality, but by implication indicates that "personality" stands for narrow, selfish, private personal events and experiences which great poetry is supposed to escape and transcend. Unless a poet becomes neutral and is indifferent to his personal experiences, he will not be able to handle these in art with balance, beauty and perfection. Art may take its origin in one's personal experience or event, but this experience or event needs to be transmuted or transformed into something richer and more complex, impersonal and universal. "Personality" in Eliot's definition stands for the selfish, the private and obscure impulses and experiences. It is another term for what Bernard Shaw calls "the little selfish clod of ailments". To be "Personal" is to be pseudo Romantic, to be oblique, muddle-headed, to be "moaning" or "whining," to be sloppy, blurred and sentimental.

Hence, Eliot's escape from personality is virtually a plea for an escape from emotionalism and narrowness. Eliot in 1919 had a determined aim to shift the centre of emphasis in the theory and practice of poetry. He wanted to divert the reader's interest from the content to the medium and the artistic process.

The point of view, which Eliot struggles to attack in "Tradition and the Individual Talent", is related to the metaphysical theory of the substantial unity of the soul. Eliot's meaning is that the poet has "not a personality" to express but a particular medium which is only a medium and not a personality....In the context of its time, it was necessary to make such an assertion for resisting and countering "the post-Swinburnian arrest", and to insist on art as art, as medium, artistic process, structure and shapeliness.

Thomas Parkinson in his essay, "Intimate and Impersonal, an

Aspect of Modern Poetics."[24] throws much light on Eliot's opinion about the escape from personality in poetry. He points out that a major work on the motives of modern art is Ortegay Gasset's *The Dehumanisation of Art*. The major motive of the new writer is to purify art, to be wilfully anti-popular, and to tend towards "dehumanisation". The human content should thin to such a point that the artist's loyalty should be to the inherent nature of the medium. In poetry and painting, according to the new trend, the mimetic or the non-creative part of an artist's work is the personal experience. From the viewpoint of the new art, the most that can be said for "personal experience" is that it may be the pretext of poetical composition. But the painting or poem is not to be tested by its fidelity to natural form (its realism) or to personal experience (its sincerity), for the art-work is neither representational nor reminiscent. The proper aim of the artist is to create an impersonal artifact; and this extreme stand is opposite to the realistic and personalist aesthetics of his immediate predecessors. Kandinsky, Appolinaire, Ezra Pound and others had reacted against the personalist aesthetics and the same point of view led Eliot to say, with a certain pleasure in outraging an audience, that the progress of an artist is a continual self-sacrifice. It is healthy for art sometimes to divert one's attention from content to medium or from the sincerity of experience to the making and the shaping of the poem. Eliot writes : "For it is not the greatness or the intensity of the emotions, the components, but the intensity of the artistic process, the pressure so to speak, under which the fusion takes place...."[25]

Dr. Leavis in his younger days was an active admirer of Eliot. Late in his life, however, he wrote a severe criticism of Eliot in his review "Eliot's Stature as Critic" in *Commentary* :

> ....Some of the ideas, attitudes and valuations put into currency by Eliot were arbitrary....The limitation, the disability....it is a case challenging a diagnostic approach — has its ominous document in a famous early essay : "Tradition and the Individual Talent." It was on this preeminently that was based Eliot's reputation as a thinker....

Actually Eliot's trenchancy and vigour are illusory; the essay is notable for its ambiguities, its logical inconsequence its pseudo-precisions, its fallaciousness, the aplomb of its equivocations, and its specious cogency. Its excellent compression and its technique in general for generating awed confusion help to explain why it should not have been found easy to deal with. Yet the falsity and gratuitousness of its doctrine' of impersonality are surely plain enough...."It is not then a coherent conception of art that is figured in Eliot's artist."[26]

Dr. Leavis here seems to write forcefully and brilliantly; yet his charge against Eliot, particularly his essay "Tradition and the Individual Talent," is not very substantial. Had Dr. Leavis kept the background of Eliot's essay uppermost in his mind, he would not have swooped so heavily on Eliot. The "vigour" in "Tradition and the Individual Talent" is not, as F.R. Leavis says, "illusory." Eliot, in "Tradition and the Individual Talent" and some other earlier essays, writes with great power, energy and vehemence, as some of the attitudes and ideas moved Eliot the poet also. There may not be whole truth (and who has found the whole truth?) in the earlier essays of Eliot but in them he arranges his arguments and stand most vigorously. It will not be right on the part of a critic to be diffident when he has to prove to the reader a thesis almost antithetical to the prevalent one. He will have to assert, explain, elucidate, explicate thread by thread, even repeat vigorously and debate his diametrically opposed dictum to instil it in the mind of the reader.

It is surprising that Dr. Leavis in this review does not mention Eliot's developed notion of impersonality and personality which should have been fully agreeable to him.

To escape from "personality" means to check and control one's excessive overflowing emotion and to transmute it into universal, impersonal art that it may not seem to bear the trace of private experience. Eliot writes relevantly in a review, entitled "The Problem of the Shakespeare's Sonnets" :

> Nowhere is the public in general more at fault than in its decipherings of the meaning of poems according to some experience." A fine poem which appears to be the record of a particular experience may be the work of a man who has never had that experience; a poem

which is the record of a particular experience may bear
no trace of that or of any experience.

About good poetry the public....is usually quite wrong;
the experience it sees behind the poem is its own, not
the poet's. I do not say that poetry is not
"autobiographical" but this autobiography is written by
a foreign tongue, which can never be translated....

The greater the verse, the less it seems to belong to the
individual man who wrote it.[27]

In good and great poetry there is always a curb on the
emotions and the petty and the particular are extended to the
universal. A piece of art may take its origin in the personal, private
feelings and emotions of the artist but this personal feeling or the
"personality" is transformed into something rich and strange as if
the bones are made coral. Eliot writes :

Shakespeare, too, was occupied with the struggle which alone
constitutes life for a poet — to transmute his personal and private
agonies into something rich and strange, something universal and
impersonal. The rage of Dante against Florence or what not, the
deep surge of Shakespeare's general, cynicism and disillusionment
are merely gigantic attempts to metamorphose private failure and
disappointments.[28]

The mind of the poet, as Eliot says, is the shred of platinum.
It may operate upon the experience of the man himself but it should
remain neutral and unchanged, like the platinum, and then only is
there the possibility of good art. Eliot has given a memorable and
epochmaking expression by saying, "the more perfect the artist,
the more completely separate in him will be the man who suffers
and the mind which creates." Eliot is right. While creating art a
man is required to keep his mind serene, however, harrowing
and violent the experience. A great artist is not the servant but
the master of his material. The perfect artist is a great deal
separate from the suffering man in him in the sense that the artist
has to be neutral in order to master, control, organise and
transmute his sufferings into art. Hence, we are reminded of the
lines of Eliot's dissertation which explain and cast further light
on Eliot's idea of the poet's mind as platinum :

To say that one part of the mind suffers and another part reflects upon the suffering is perhaps to talk in fictions. But we know that those highly organised beings who are able to objectify their passions, and as passive spectators to contemplate their joys and torments, are also those who suffer and enjoy the most keenly.[29]

F.R. Leavis criticises Eliot's idea about the separation between the "man who suffers" and "the mind which creates" :

This, plausible or discussible as it might for a moment seem, is a wholly arbitrary dictum....The analogy of the catalyst gives it no support (all it does is to make the underlying intention plain).[30]

And someone in *The Criterion*[31] has also pointed out that Eliot's scientific presentation of the argument in support of his thesis is mathematically incorrect. He deplores that Eliot in writing or revising the essay "Tradition and the Individual Talent" did not consult a professional chemist or a friend with elementary knowledge of chemistry. On page 17 line 25 in Selected Essay she takes oxygen and sulphur-dioxide and on page 18, lines 9-11, he produces sulphurous acid from them. O_2 Plus $2SO_2$ do not equal $2H_2SO_3$ but only $2SO_3$, which in the presence of water gives SO_3 plus $H_2O = H_2SO_4$ sulphuric acid.

There is, of course, a catalytic reaction involving platinum and one of the sulphur gases, but Eliot, being stparated from the library, cannot quote the exact terms and conditions available in any book of inorganic chemistry.

Aristotle's discussion of the nature of the soul (particularly *De Anima* 408b 13-32) seems to have clearly influenced the general scheme of the essay, "Tradition and the Individual Talent". Eliot has quoted a tag from Aristotle as epigraph in Section III of this essay.

In the lines quoted by Eliot, Aristotle says "the mind is something more god-like, and is unaffected", or, for the Greek word has several nuances, "indifferent", or-without suffering."

The notion of impersonality or the principle of depersonalization in art as shown in "Tradition and the individual Talent" seems to us somewhat rigid and mechanical, like the geometrical line of T.E. Hulme's *Speculations*. Eliot brings to us the most developed, extended and profound conception of "impersonality in his essay on W.B. Yeats. He means to say in this essay that ,impersonality", with which he was engaged some years earlier, was more or less of the mechanical or of the inferior kind. The really great impersonal poetry of which Eliot became more clearly aware later on, can result only when there is enough of the personal or felt experience behind the poet. The great "impersonality is outwardly cool like the tranquil surface of an ocean but it is raging, turbulent beneath the surface. Behind the immense force and power of Swift's work, there is the feel of the constant vital transmission of the personality — Swift's disappointments and despairs, either in the political sphere or in a love-affair. Thus Swift is in an adequate position to do ruthless, powerful, passionate condemnation of humanity and the world. The personal cynicism, the disgust, the contempt have been metamorphosed into an impersonal mask. Eliot points out that there are two kinds of impersonality achieved by the artist in his art ; one is of the inferior kind — the impersonality of a mere craftsman — and the other is the impersonality of the first order, impersonality forged out of intense personal emotion and passion. While introducing *Le Serpent* of Paul Valéry, Eliot expresses a similar thought :

> Like all of Valéry's poetry, it is impersonal in the sense that personal emotion, personal experience is extended and completed in something impersonal — not in the sense of something divorced from personal experience and passion....

Eliot's developed notion of impersonality deserves to be quoted in full :

> ....but I think now at least that the truth of the matter [the problem of personality and impersonality] is as follows There are two forms of imipersonality : that which is natural to the mere skilful craftsman, and that which is more and more achieved by the maturing artist. The first is that of which I have called the anthology piece, of a lyric by Lovelace or Suckling or of Campion, a finer poet than either. The second impersonality is that of the poet who out of intense and personal experience, is able to express a general truth; retaining all the

particularity of his experience to make of it a general symbol.[32]

Poetry is both the particularization of the universal and the universalisation of the particular.

Eliot's notion of the historical sense or the traditional sense is somehow linked up with the idea of poetry as "escape from emotion" and "escape from personality". The sense of tradition Eliot intends to express, is a means of control over one's excessive, "personalism". It enables the poet to see and interpret his experience in terms of the experiences of other writers and ages. Eliot praises the utmost honesty, truthfulness and the naked vision of Blake's poetry but deplores the lack of traditional or historical sense which might have countered the esoteric part of his thought and vision.

To be traditional in Eliot's sense, however, means also to have read and studied the significant works of the greater writers and to be aware of all past literature. To be traditional is equal to having mastered the other masters and to be allusive. It is to render, interpret and illuminate the present in the light of the vision of the past masters.

"Unreal city...."

Here the words, as is well-known, are operating on different levels simultaneously, in terms of Dante's Limbo and Baudelaire's nightmare city. The insistence on the traditional is more important for a critic than for a poet.

Regarding the concept of tradition, he wants that one should not be guided by poetry of one age only, for example, the nineteenth century. Hence, Eliot adopts a corrective attitude to set right the reader's taste and make it comprehensive :

> ....I have met but very few people in my life 'who really care for poetry and those few, when they have the knowledge (for they are sometimes quite illiterate people) know how to take from every poet what he has to give, and reject only those poets who whatever they give always pretend to give more than they do give; these discerning people appreciate the work of Pope and Dryden (indeed it might be said in our time

that the man who cannot enjoy Pope as poetry probably understands no poetry)....[33]

Eliot has a coherent conception of poetry. He feels that poetry is good and effective only when emotion and intellect combine and cohere. In a good poem passion and reasoning, delicacy and logic should unite or go side by side or reinforce each other. Eliot is fond of English Metaphysical poetry because he finds there both reasoning and passion in unison.

He says that a thought to Donne was an experience. Good poetry is the recreation of thought. A good poet in Eliot's sense feels his thoughts as immediately as the odour of a rose. His mode of feeling is directly and freshly altered by reading and thought. Whatever the subject-matter — the reading of Spinoza, the smell of the gutter, the noise of the typewriter, or the experience of loving a girl — if the poet has the basic passionate, sensitive, amalgamating faculty, his poetry will not go dry. Poetry, Eliot says, is the emotional equivalent of thought. Eliot is not a dry classicist who is in favour of discarding emotion. Often the emotional in a poem or a piece of art is the cause of Eliot's choice and commendation. In his essay "Poetry and Propaganda", he presents the notion of good poetry as "thinking through feeling" or "feeling through thinking...." And in his essay "Shakespeare and the Stoicism of Seneca" Eliot says that what every poet starts from, is his own emotion. At another place he writes that the keenest ideas have the quality of sense perception. While introducing Kipling's verse, Eliot opines, that the first condition of right thought is right sensation.

"Dissociation of sensibility" happens in poetry usually when only one aspect of sensibility is exercised to the complete neglect of the other aspect. Eliot wants poetry to 'present the complete unity and the fullest reality that we encounter in the "Immediate Experience" of F.H. Bradley. In "Immediate Experience" reason and emotion are resolved.

While discussing Eliot's aesthetic of verse it is essential to explain "dissociation of sensibility" at length. Eliot is himself surprised at the unexpected reputation that this phrase has earned. "Dissociation of sensibility" means much or almost nothing as it points to a quite general, common, basic feature of any good poem. It is not wholly a new term, though no previous critic had laid this much emphasis on this point and in such novel, memorable phrasing. This term stands generally for the separation of feeling from thinking, intellect from passion. But in fact at no stage and in no poem (good or bad) is there merely thinking or merely feeling. Eliot writes in his doctoral dissertation : "No stage can be so low as to be mere feeling...."[34]

Eliot's "dissociation of sensibility" and unification of sensibility, are all implicit in Coleridge's concept of Imagination and seem to have been fathered by it.

"Dissociation of sensibility" is not an evil that a poet must escape or avoid at his discretion. It is to be taken simply as the resulting feature of a bad poem. In poetry, a poet does not bring unification of sensibility by deliberation; rather he brings it into his poem most naturally. "Dissociation of sensibility" takes place specially when one feature or quality in a poem is emphasised and refined at the cost of the other. It points also to the imbalance between the refinement of language and the degree of feeling; fancy and the matter-of-factness; the auditory and the visual. It suggests also the feeling not done through thinking, and *vice versa*. Dissociation of sensibility may also result from one's vast learning of multifarious subjects without any passionate digestion and apprehension of these subjects.

The term "dissociation of sensibility" is directly dwelt upon in Eliot's essays on Milton, Marvell, and in "The Metaphysical Poets" :

> It is interesting to speculate whether it is not a misfortune that two of the greatest masters of diction in our language, Milton and Dryden, trinmph with dazzling disregard of the soul.[35]

And more :

> The two greatest masters of diction [Racine and Baudelaire] are also the greatest two psychologists, the most curious explorers of the soul.[36]

That Eliot quotes Coleridge on Imagination in his essay on Marvell should be regarded as a clue to Eliot's term "dissociation of sensibility." Eliot wants that poetry should be conceived and composed not only in the soul but also in the cerebral cortex, the nervous system and the digestive tracts. When a poet's sensibility is dissociated, language inevitably becomes crippled and certain special properties are refined and cultivated while others are atrophied.

"Dissociation of sensibility" is derived, as F.W. Bateson boints out,[37] from a passage in Rémy de Gourmont's essay on Laforgue. There, Rémy de Gourmont argues that intelligence and sensibility in a man of original genius like Laforgue are "the flowering of one physiology."

For Eliot, poetry is neither pure cerebration nor simple sensation but the integration of both.

Eliot has added admirably to the fund of critical terminology by distinguishing poetry from verse. There are normally three terms — poetry, verse and prose — but while introducing *Anabasis*, a poem of St. John Perse, Eliot says there should be four. The opposite of poetry is not always verse. A good impersonal poem of some length cannot be written by a poet unless he is a master of verse and the prosaic also. Eliot does not agree with Poe that a long poem is a contradiction in terms. What Poe wants is "distilled poetry" of equal intensity from the first line to the last. Eliot, on the other hand, insists that there should be some transition or variation between the lines of higher pitch and those of the lower one. A poet should combine both verse and poetry in a poem. Eliot has dispelled the derogatory association with "minor poetry" and —"verse". He says that in poetry there are many casements which are not magic and poetry is not always liquid sentiment poured over in a ready made mould. Eliot writes while introducing St. John Perse's poem :

> Poetry may occur within a definite limit on one side at any point along a line of which the formal limits are verse and prose; without offering any generalized theory about poetry, verse and prose I may suggest that a writer by using, as does Mr. Perse, certain exclusively poetic methods, is sometimes able to write poetry in what is called prose....As a matter of fact, much bad poetic prose and a very small part of bad verse is bad because it is prosaic.

Eliot casts more light on the problem while introducing the poems of Pound :

> One cannot write poetry all the time ; and when one cannot write poetry, it is better to write what one knows is verse and make it good verse, than to write bad verse and persuade oneself that it is good poetry.

In his essay on Dryden, Eliot says that the prospect of delight above all justifies the perusal of poetry.

Language naturally is Eliot's major concern. He realised that a new language or new diction needs to be forged after any alteration in sensibility. The language which is more important to us, is that which is struggling to digest and express new objects, new feelings and new aspects. He insists that the language of poetry should keep abreast of the speech rhythm of its time. Milton's language in general has not the vitality and verve of speech rhythm. It has not the muscular tension and the sensory rhythm of Shakespeare. Language in a healthy state presents the object, it is so close to the object that the two are identified. And Eliot says that a poet's function is to purify, develop and enrich the dialect of the tribe.

Ultimately, Eliot wants for poetry some system of thought, some coherent plausible thread of belief, some vision or point of view. That is why Eliot is fascinated by Dante in whose work he finds economy of language and a system of thought. Eliot insists on the study of the whole work of an author, as only in sequence and totality can we have an idea of the point of view forming or developing in a particular writer. One of the marks of the greatness of a writer is whether his works taken as a whole bring to us more than what they do when read piecemeal. This bias for some point of view in a work of art is the reason that Eliot has been drawn to the conclusion that in appreciating art he cannot suspend or neutralize his personal belief. Dante for Eliot has everything in his poetry : simplicity and lucidity of style, precision and economy of presentation, "the greatest altitude and greatest depth of human passion", and a system of thought. Hence, to Eliot, Dante presents a saner attitude to life. In "Religion and Literature", Eliot opines that the greatness of literature is to be judged not by literary standards alone.

The persons who enjoy these writings solely because of their literary merit are essentially parasites....I could fulminate against the men of letters who have gone into ecstasies over the Bible as literature....[38]

In art, Eliot, like Henry James, wants some figure in the carpet. He says that pure poetry is a phantom and that both in creation and enjoyment, much always enters which is, from the point of view of art, irrelevant. Eliot modestly calls it a personal prejudice of his that he takes the greatest pleasure in poetry with a clear philosophical pattern. The great poet, he continues has something to say — something which is over and above the verbal beauty. In "Goethe as the Sage" Eliot writes : "....that the wisdom and the poetry are inseparable, in the poets of the highest rank, is something I have only come to perceive in becoming a little wiser myself."[39]

REFERENCES

1. *Selected Essays*, p. 21.
2. *To Criticise the Critic*, p. 16.
3. Eliot's Introduction, *Savonarola*, a dramatic poem by Charlotte Eliot, xi.
4. *Literary Opinion in America*, Vol. 2, edited by M.D. Zabel, p. 573.
5. *Selected Essays*, p. 22.
6. *Essays in Criticism* (2nd series), Macmillan, 1958, pp. 56-57.
7. *Selected* Essays, p. 290.
8. *Ibid.*, p. 21.
9. *Ibid.*, p. 18.
10. *Principles of Literary Criticism*, Routledge & Kegan Paul, p. 6.
11. *Ibid.*, p. 10.
12. "The Silurist", a review by Eliot, *Dial*, LXXXIII, 3 (September. 1927), 259-68.
13. *The Sacred Wood*, pp. 147-48.
14. Quoted by Eliot, *To Criticise the Critic*, p. 175.
15. *To Criticise the Critic*, p. 170.
16. David Daiches, *The Present Age*, pp. 123-24.
17. *Speculations*, p. 96.
18. *Dial*, November 1923.
19. Eliot, *Knowledge and Experience*, p. 24.
20. *Ibid.*, p. 23.
21. *Selected Essays*, p. 21.

22. *Ibid.,* p. 22.
23. *Ibid.*
24. *Journal of Aesthetics and Art Criticism,* XVI, Nov. 3, March 1958.
25. *Selected Essays,* p. 19.
26. *Commentary, XXVI,* Nov. 1958, p. 400.
27. *Nation and Athenaeum,* XLV, 19, Feb. 1927, p. 18.
28. *Selected Essays,* p. 137.
29. Eliot, *Knowledge and Experience,* p. 23.
30. F.R. Leavis, "Eliot's Stature as Critic," *Commentary, XXVI,* Nov. 1958, p. 400.
31. *The Criterion,* Vol. XH, No. 46, October 1932, p. 167.
32. W.B. Yeats, *On Poetry and Poets,* p. 255.
33. Eliot's Introduction, *Selected Poems of Pound;* included also in Pound, edited by J.P. Sullivan. pp. 107-08.
34. *Knowledge and Experience,* p. 18.
35. Selected Prose, edited by John Hayward, p. 120.
36. *Ibid.*
37. F.W. Bateson, "Dissociation of Sensibility", *Essays in Criticism,* July 1951.
38. *Selected Prose,* p. 33.
39. *On Poetry and Poets,* p. 195.

4

The Function and Frontiers of Criticism

Before we define criticism in Eliot's terms, we may like to know the origin and the history of the words "criticism" and "critic". "Critic" has been derived from the Greek word "kritikos", which means a judge of literature. "Kritikos" occurs in writings almost at the end of the century B.C. Its place was taken by a new word "criticus" which aimed at the interpretation of texts and words, and improvement of the works of writers in either Greek or Latin.

The words "criticism" and "critic" hardly occur in English in the Elizabethan age. The word "critic" never occurs in the anthology by Gregory Smith of Elizabethan critical essays; it is used only in Bacon's *Advancement of Learning* (1605).

The word "criticism" was used, in the modern sense, by Dryden in his preface to *The State of Innocence* (1677). He wrote, "Criticism, as it was first instituted by Aristotle, was meant a standard of judging well." With Pope's Essay *on Criticism* (1711) the term "criticism" was firmly established in English. Today, the term Literary Criticism is applied to the study of works of literature with emphasis on their valuation.

In different contexts and on different occasions Eliot has defined the nature and function of criticism :

(1) Criticism is the elucidation of works of art and the correction of literary taste.[1]

(2) The function of criticism is to promote the understanding and enjoyment of literature.[2]

(3) To bring the past back to life is the great perennial
     task of criticism.

(4) A critic's task is "to detect the living from the dead."

(5) The rudiment of criticism is the ability to select a good
     poet and reject a bad one.[3]

(6) One function of criticism is to act as a kind of cog
     regulating the rate of change in literary taste.[4]

(7) The good critic is the man who, to a keen and abiding
     sensibility, joins wide and increasingly discriminating
     reading.

(8) It is part of the business of a critic to preserve tradition
     where a good tradition exists It is part of his business
     to see literature steadily and to see it whole; and this
     is eminently to see it not as consecrated by time, but
     to see it beyond time; to see the best work of our
     time and the best work of twenty five hundred years
     ago with the same eyes.[5]

(9) Criticism is said to be "the common pursuit of
     true judgement."

(10) "It would appear that criticism, like any pbilosophical
     activity, is inevitable and requires no justification....You
     cannot deplore criticism unless you deprecate philosophy."[6]

Elsewhere Eliot defines criticism as F.H. Bradley says of
metaphysics : "the finding of bad reasons for what we believe
upon instinct, but to find these reasons is no less an instinct."[7] A
favourite quotation of Eliot is from Rémy de Gourmont that the
critic's task is "eriger en lois ses impréssions personnelles" *(i.e.,*
to convert personal impressions into the appearance of an abstract
and universal idea). Eliot in a review dwells upon a critic's
requirements : .

> Analysis and comparison methodically with sensitiveness,
> intelligence, curiosity, intensity of passion and infinite
> knowledge; all these are necessary to the great critic.
> Comparison, the periodical public does not want much
> of; it does not like to be made to feel that it ought to
> have read much more than it has read before it can
> follow the critic's thought; analysis it is afraid of.[8]

In order to grasp the real earnestness behind Eliot's notions of criticism we should take note of his distinction of criticism from interpretation. Interpretation, in Eliot's opinion, is not tantamount to proper criticism. In his essay "The Function of Criticism", he is definitely antipathetic to it. He says that proper criticism of a particular piece of art is supposed to enable the reader to be possessed of facts, but a critic should be the master and not the servant of facts. Eliot has a tendency to suspect interpretation : "And for every success in this type of writing there are thousands of impostors. Instead of insight, you get a fiction."[9] And further : "But it is fairly certain that interpretation (I am not touching upon the acrostic element in literature) is only legitimate when it is not interpretation at all, but merely putting the reader in possession of facts which he would otherwise have missed."[10]

There is a species of interpretative commentary from which literary criticism is almost absent. The danger here is that the commentator, falling in love afresh with his own ideas and theories, will drift farther and farther away from the work which he is supposedly elucidating and that the trusting reader who follows him will be unable to get back to that work. The reader is left with the immovable opaque block of the commentary, and what little he has received of the original work has been emasculated and predigested, instead of gained through personal effort. The usual critical procedure of fairly constant reference to the text is the only safeguard against this very human weakness, After many years, while writing an introduction to *The Wheel of Fire* by Wilson Knight, Eliot reveals himself as less intolerant of the rightness, validity and the usefulness of interpretation.

He concedes "interpretation" to be a natural, instinctive, legitimate and necessary urge of man. He says that the restless demon in us drives us to. interpret, whether we will or not :

> To interpret then or to seek to pounce upon the secret, to elucidate the pattern and pluck out the mystery of a poet's work, is no less an instinct. Nor is the effort altogether vain; for as the study of philosophy, and indeed the surrendering of oneself, with adequate knowledge of other systems, some systems of our own or of someone else, is as needful a part of man's life

as falling in love or making any contract, so it is
necessary to surrender ourselves to some interpretation
of the poetry we like.

And I do not mean that nothing solid and enduring
can be arrived at in interpretation; but it seems to me
that there must be as a matter of fact in every effort
of interpretation, some part which can be accepted and
necessarily also some part which other writers can
reject....Without pursuing that curious and obscure
problem of the meaning of interpretation farther, it
occurs to me as possible that there may be an essential
part of error in all interpretation, without which it will
not be interpretation at all....

Professor Wilson Knight also, while highlighting the principles
of Shakespearean interpretation in *The Wheel* of *Fire,* makes the
right distinction between criticism and interpretation and says that
criticism suggests to him a certain process of deliberately
objectifying the work under consideration; the comparison of it
with other similar works, in order, specially, to show in what
respects it surpasses or falls short of those works; then dividing
its good from its bad; and finally, a formal judgment as to its
lasting validity. Interpretation on the contrary tends to merge into
the work it analyses, it attempts as far as possible to understand
its subject in the light of its own nature. It avoids discussion of
merits. Wilson Knight further says :

Thus, criticism is active and looks ahead, often treating
past work as material on which to base future standards
and canons of art; interpretation is passive, and looks
back, regarding only the imperative challenge of a poetic
vision.

Criticism is a judgement of vision; interpretation a recon-
struction of vision. It is probable that neither can exist, quite
divorced from the other. Coleridge, Hazlitt and A.C. Bradley have
the interpretative approach mainly.

Eliot's early review entitled "Beyle and Balzac"[11] is more an
interpretation than a piece of criticism :

It is this intensity, precisely, and consequent discontent
with the inevitable inadequacy of actual living to the
passionate capacity, which drove them to art and

analysis. The surface of existence coagulates into lumps, which look like important simple feelings, which are identified by names as feeling, which the patient analyst disintegrates into more complex or trifling, but ultimately if he goes far enough, into various canalisations of something again simple, terrible and unknown.[12]

As critical statements, these are illuminating, but not in the way in which Eliot, in "The Function of Criticism", said that criticism should be. They have really got nothing to do with facts, but describe in a highly subjective and rhetorical way, a felt relationship between Eliot and the two great French novelists. This kind of criticism is, in the strictest sense, interpretation, a paraphrasing of meaning and significance in terms of the creative context in which the artist works.

Eliot's essays on Marvell, Blake, Swinburne, Ezra Pound and some others are criticism proper as in these essays we find the procedure of comparison and analysis, direct inquiry and examination of text, and disinterested assessment. "From Poe to Valéry" also as a piece of proper criticism is of the first order. Eliot remarks brilliantly regarding "The Raven" of Poe :

> The bird is addressed as no craven, quite needlessly, except for the pressing need of rhyme to "raven" — a surrender to the exigencies of rhyme with which I am sure Malherbe would have had no patience.[13]

His criticism of Swinburne is equally trenchant :

You see that Provenee is the merest point of diffusion here. Swinburne defines the place by the most general word, which has for him its own value. Gold, ruin, dolorous; it is not merely the sound that he wants but the vague associations of idea that the words give him. He has not his eye on a particular place....It is in fact the word that gives him the thrill, not the object.[14]

The critical essays of Eliot like "The Function of Criticism". "The Frontiers of Criticism" and "The Experiment in Criticism" represent the ideals of true criticism. In "The Function of Criticism" there is an ire against impressionistic or aesthetic criticism and a wrangle with Middleton Murry's "Inner Voice". True criticism aims always at objectivity and springs directly from the text, and generalization is immediately relevant to it. For the pursuit of objectivity in criticism some guide-line or authority should be acknowledged, for constant listening to one's inner voice will lead one to fancy or fiction or sheer subjectivity and make criticism otiose. Eliot is very critical of Middleton Murry's statement : "The English writer, the English divine, the English statesman inherit no rules from their forbears; they inherit only this; a sense that in the last resort they must depend upon the inner voice" — and says that "inner voice" in criticism will not work, it will rather lead the critic astray as it is equal to "doing as one likes". Eliot terms this "inner voice" also as "whiggery" or "muddle through."

Middleton Murry repudiates the principles of Catholicism as well as classicism, but for Eliot, there is some kinship or common thread passing between them and criticism. Eliot writes ironically of Middleton Murry's inner voice :

> Why have principles, when one has the inner voice? If I like a thing, that is all I want; and if enough of us shouting all together, like it, that should be all that you (who do not like it) ought to want. The law of art, said Mr. Clutton Brock, is all case law And we cannot only like whatever we like to like, but we can like it for any reason we choose.[15]

In "The Function of Criticism", Eliot has uttered many other useful points of permanent validity concerning criticism and critics. Here be defines criticism as "the commentation and exposition of works of art by means of written words". He says that criticism is not an autotelic activity nor the critic a "palpitating Narcissus."[16] The traditional sense or the historical sense is more essential for a critic rather than for a poet. Comparison and analysis, Rémy de Gourmont had said before Eliot, are the chief tools of a critic. It is obvious indeed that they are tools to be handled with care. And a critic should have a highly developed sense of fact; that is why scholarship, even in its humblest forms, has its rights. Eliot says :

> and any book, any essays, any note in *Notes and Queries,* which produces a fact even of the lowest order about a work of art is a better piece of work than nine-tenth of the most pretentious critical journalism, in journals or books....Facts cannot corrupt taste....The real

corrupters are those who supply opinion or fancy. And Goethe and Coleridge are not guiltless — for what is Coleridge's Hamlet; is it an honest inquiry as far as the data permit or is it an attempt to present Coleridge in an attractive costume?[17]

A critic should try his best to overcome his prejudices and whims in order to have poise, balance, truth and objectivity in his criticism. Eliot writes in this context :

> The critic, one would suppose, if he is to justify his existence, should endeavour to discipline his personal prejudices and cranks — tares to which we are all subject — and compose his differences with as many of his fellows as possible in the common pursuit of true judgment.[18]

Eliot focuses a great deal of light on the terms called "critical" and "creative" and says that it is unwise to distinguish too bluntly between the two activities. Critical toil done consciously or unconsciously is implied in creation, as no good art is possible without it. The better creative artist is often more "critical" than the inferior one. If we find no apparent critical labour in a creative work, we should not conclude that it has been or is good without it, as we do not know what previous labours have prepared, or what goes in the way of criticism, all the time in the minds of creators. And one should note further that there is a place for criticism in creation but not *vice versa*, and that creative criticism, in the usual and general sense, has no positive use and justification. Eliot says :

> I have assumed as axiomatic that a creation, a work of art, is autotelic; and that criticism by definition, is about something other than itself. Hence you cannot fuse creation with criticism as you can fuse criticism with creation.[19]

Eliot's "The Frontiers of Criticism" may be called a classic essay on criticism. In "The Function of Criticism" Eliot favours scholarship and the finding of facts — of even the lowest order— and distrusts interpretation. The discovery of Shakespeare's laundry bills, as Eliot suggests, may have no use for us but may be put to some use by men of genius in the distant future. Hence, one should not pass hasty judgement on any scholarship of even the humblest form. But later on Eliot finds that this kind of fact-finding and research-doing has been alarmingly extended by the critics, and consequently the understanding and enjoyment of poetry and art, which should have come first, has receded to the background.

The finding of the genesis of a poem began to be misunderstood for "understanding". By seeking the source and the origin of a work of art one cannot have the right understanding and criticism of it. A critic's task, Eliot reiterates, is "to promote understanding and enjoyment" of art. He says that too much of detail about a poet or a poem of the biographical, political or sociological kind, may often bring a barrier to our immediate understanding and apprehension of the vital experience and the glow of poetry. In *Road to Xanadu,* Livingston Lowes, for example, has found details of the obscure books from which Coleridge is held to have borrowed images or phrases for his poems, "Kubla Khan" and "The Ancient Mariner", but some readers erroneously take this book, or "fascinating piece of detection", as the real clue to Coleridge's poetry. But in fact this detection does not actually enhance or add to our understanding and enjoyment of Coleridge's poetry itself. How those images and phrases were moulded into poetry remains as much a mystery as ever. Eliot holds himself somewhat guilty for the development of an unhealthy trend in criticism. He says his Notes to *The Waste Land* led critics and readers to a wrong kind of notion — probably the notion of criticism by source and the understanding of poem by genesis. But he had added Notes to the well-known poem, he informs us, just to increase the number of printed pages.

Herbert Read in his book on Wordsworth explains the rise and fall of Wordsworth's genius in terms of his love affair with Annette Vallon. And F.W. Bateson discovers that Annette Vallon does not count so much as Wordsworth's love for his own sister, Dorothy. This explains, in particular, as Eliot acknowledges, the Lucy poems, and explains why, after Wordsworth's marriage, his inspiration dried up. This argument, he says, is plausible but the real question remains : does this account help the reader to understand the Lucy poems any better than he did before? Eliot on his part does not feel helped by this biographical discovery :

For myself I can only say that a knowledge of the
springs which released a poem is not necessarily a help
towards understanding the poem; too much information
about the origins of the poem may even break my
contact with it. I feel no need for any light upon the
Lucy poems beyond the radiance shed by the poems
themselves....I am even prepared to suggest that there
is, in all great poetry, something which must remain
unaccountable however complete might be our
knowledge of the poet, and that is what matters most.
When the poem has been made, something new has
happened, something that cannot be wholly explained
by *anything that went before*. That, I believe, is what
we mean by "creation."[20]

Eliot states further that he understands some poetry without
explanation, for instance, Shakespeare's "Full fathom five thy father
lies" or Shelley's "Art thou pale for weariness/of climbing heaven
and gazing on the earth."

Here and in a great deal of other poetry, Eliot sees nothing to
be explained, nothing, that is, that would help him understand it
better and therefore enjoy it more. And for enjoyment and
understanding every book of poetry does not need a great deal of
dissection. The enigmas provided *by Finnegans Wake* have given
support to the error, prevalent nowadays, of mistaking explanation
for understanding. And sometimes, as Eliot says, explanation can
distract us from the poem as poetry.

Eliot derides critics who have stepped out of the limits of
literary criticism and are doing the work of biography, philosophy
or sociology under the guise of scholarship and fact-finding. Such
critics should better be called historians, sociologists or
philosophers. There are limits, exceeding which, in one direction,
literary criticism ceases to be literary, and exceeding which, in
another, it ceases to be criticism. The writing of critical biography
is a very delicate task. One is likely to be misled or tempted to
write more biography than criticism. The biographer of an author
should possess some critical ability and a critic in order to
understand the work of an author should have some knowledge
of his biography.

To a great extent, he can be called an empirical critic who learns and acts by experience. He aspires not only to the formulation of timeless principles but also responds to the needs of a particular time. There can be a time, when Milton's language cannot help us in keeping language colloquial and natural, but at another time it can be useful and beneficial to the language by preventing it from being changed too rapidly. In the same vein Eliot says :

> Thirty-three years ago it seemed to have been the latter type of criticism, the impressionistic, that had caused the annoyance I felt when I wrote "The Function of Criticism". Today, it seems to me that we need to be more on guard against the purely explanatory.[21]

The difference between the literary critic and the critic who has passed beyond the frontier of literary criticism is not that the literary critic has very limited interest or no interest beyond literature, for such a critic in that case will have very little to say to us. A critic is not supposed to be merely a technical expert, only to see some rules to be observed by a poet. The critic should be the whole man "with conviction and principles, and knowledge and experience of life" to recognise duly the richness, variety and depth of the experience and the moral vision of the artist. A technical critic may be called only one-fourth a critic. Eliot insists on the task of a critic as "the promotion of enjoyment and understanding" of a work of art. A critic should not be only a technical or verbal expert. But enjoyment and understanding of poetry do not come often by themselves, by studying a poem on the printed page. Henry James made a very significant statement regarding the nature and role of a critic : "Woe to the mere official critic, the critic who has never felt the man."[22]

At present there has been development of numerous sciences like semantics, anthropology, aesthetics, and so on, and different branches of specialization are possible. Consequently, the frontiers of literary criticism are in greater likelihood of being blurred.

But among all this variety, asks Eliot, what is there, if anything, that should be common to all literary criticism?

Eliot feels that literary criticism cannot keep itself aloof or separated from the developments and numerous happenings of the present. Many sciences will have their impact on literature and criticism. Hence, "the transformation of criticism"[23] cannot be deplored completely. But Eliot insists that literary criticism in the right sense should be "literary." To be literary, as he explains his point, does not mean to be limited in one's interest. It does not forbid us "to have interest beyond literature." At the same time criticism should not be a substitute for sociology, history or neurosis. The task of criticism in modern times, says Eliot in his essay, "Experiment in Criticism,"[24] is not only to expand its borders but to clarify its centre — and the insistency of the latter need grows with that of the former.

Eliot differentiates between the older literary criticism of the seventeenth and eighteenth centuries and the modern criticism, and finds a good feature in the former in that it recognises literature as literature and not another thing. Literature is something distinct from philosophy and psychology and every other study, and its purpose is to give a refined pleasure to persons of sufficient leisure and breeding. If the earlier critics had not taken for granted that literature was something primarily to be enjoyed, they could not have occupied themselves so sedulously with laying down rules of what was right to enjoy. Eliot says further in this context :

> For the earlier period, art and literature were not the substitute of religion or philosophy or morals or Politics, any more than for duelling or love-making : they were special and limited adornments of life. On each side there is profit and loss. We have gained perhaps a deeper insight, now and then; whether we enjoy literature any more keenly than our ancestors, I do not know, but I think we should return again and again to the critical writings of the seventeenth and eighteenth centuries, to remind ourselves of the simple truth that literature is primarily literature, a means of refined and intellectual pleasure."[25]

At one stage of his career Eliot attached importance to the criticism of persons who are themselves writers or artists. Later Eliot modified his opinion. Yet he rates the "notes on the art of writing by practitioners" very highly :

> But from the Renaissance through the eighteenth century, literary criticism had been confined to two

narrow, and closely related types. One was a type which can always have great value, it may be called practical notes on the art of writing by practitioners....Such notes are of the greatest value to other artists, particularly when studied in conjunction with the author's own work. Two classical examples in English are the Elizabethan treatises on rhymed and unrhymed verse written by Thomas Campion and Samuel Daniel. The prefaces and essays of Dryden, the prefaces of Corneille are of the same type but on a large scale and engage wider issues."[26]

Some part of Eliot's criticism should be called "practical notes on the art of writing" or what Eliot describes as "workshop-criticism". We know well that this kind of criticism has obvious limitations : it is revealing but limited in its range....The "practical note" does not have generality or universality. It cannot illuminate the problems or aspects of art in which a particular poet is not interested. A particular practitioner is the master of his own field; the other fields in art are beyond his competence. Thus, the workshop-criticism has definiteness but narrowness too. The ideal criticism, as Eliot states rightly, results from the collaboration of critics of various special training :

The present age has been rather uncritical and partly for economic causes. The critic has been chiefly the reviewer, that is to say, the hurried amateur wage-slave. I am aware of the danger that the types of criticism in which I am interested may become too professional and technical. What I hope for is the collaboration of critics of various special training, and perhaps the pooling and sorting of their contributions by men who will be neither specialist not amateurs.[27]

Eliot in his essays — "The Perfect Critic" and "Imperfect Critics" — deals admirably with the features of a good and a bad critic. The task of a critic, he says, is not only to point out the virtues of a writer but also to expose the fake and the fraudulent and condemn them. It is to train us not to enjoy a bad poem. Eliot takes Aristotle, Rémy de Gourmont, Rochefoucauld and Coleridge as ideal and "perfect" critics. The ideal critical faculty, as Eliot points out, consists in looking solely and steadfastly at the object and it provides us an eternal example of intelligence.[28] The perfect criticism is termed differently in different phrases as "intelligence....swiftly operating" or "the analysis of sensation to the point of principle and definition."[29] Its function is regarded simply as elucidation and the reader is to form his own correct judgment. The ideal critical mind is said to be the scientific or intelligent mind or the mind of universal intelligence which sees the object as it really, is. The best criticism means virtually "the disinterested exercise of intelligence."[30]

Eliot says, "Thus, we aim to see the object as it really is and find a meaning for the words of Arnold."[31]

The perfect critical sensibility inheres in free intelligence, and free intelligence is that which is wholly devoted to inquiry. An ideal critic like Rémy de Gourmont is said to have combined, to a remarkable degree, sensitiveness, erudition, the sense of fact and the sense of history, and generalizing power. The imperfect critic is usually emotional, impressionistic (in the bad sense) and is not devoted to sustained dissection, analysis and inquiry. He "alters" the object, but never "transforms" it. The study of a work of art often fecundates a bad critic's emotion to produce something new which is not criticism. Bad criticism like bad romanticism "leads its disciples only back upon themselves"[32] It lacks in balance and critical analysis. A bad critic "takes the reputations of the world too solemnly." He does not make a disinterested endeavour to know the best that is known and thought in the world. It is fatuous to say that criticism is for the sake of "creation" or creation for the sake of criticism. The bad imperfect criticism is a "mixed critical and creative reaction." The bad critic is like the sentimental person, in whom a work of art arouses all sorts of emotions which have nothing to do with that work of art whatever but are accidents of personal association. His criticism is "the satisfaction of a suppressed creative wish." Eliot points out the function of a perfect critic : But a literary critic should have no emotions except those immediately provoked by a work of art and these (as I have already hinted) are, when valid, perhaps not to be called emotions at all."

Aristole is accorded superlative praise; he is cited by Eliot as not only a remarkable but a universal intelligence. That is, he could apply his intelligence to anything. The ordinary intelligence is good only for certain classes of objects. He did not use art, as some persons do, as an outlet for his suppressed egotism. He solely and steadfastly looked at the object and in his short and broken treatise he provides an ideal example. He displays much "free intelligence". And he be may be called quite "a free mind".

The earlier Eliot fights shy of fully acknowledging the greatness of Coleridge, extending ambivalent, halfhearted praise to him. In "Experiment in Criticism", Eliot calls *Biographia Literaria* "one of the wisest and silliest, the most exciting and exasperating book of criticism ever written". Eliot points out the weakness of Coleridge as critic. Coleridge has made of Hamlet a Coleridge. He is also critical of Coleridge's distinction between fancy and imagination :

> Fancy may be "no other than a mode of memory emancipated from the order of space and time"; but it seems unwise to talk of memory in connection with fancy and omit it altogether from the account of imagination. As we have learnt from Dr. Lowe's *Road to Xanadu* (if we did not know it already) memory plays a very great part in imagination and of course a much larger part than can be proved by that book....[33]

And more :

> There is so much memory in imagination that if you are to distinguish between imagination and fancy in Coleridge's way you must define the difference between memory in imagination and memory in fancy : and it is not enough to say that one dissolves, diffuses and dissipates the memories in order to recreate, while the other deals with fixities and definiteness.[34]

Eliot says that Coleridge cannot be estimated as an intelligence, "completely free". Later Eliot extends wholehearted praise to Coleridge. The brash confidence of Eliot's statement in "The Function of Criticism" that Coleridge belongs among the corrupters of taste, has completely disappeared by 1956 when Eliot declares modern criticism to be in direct descent from Coleridge. Eliot further praises Coleridge for having established the critical relevance of philosophy, aesthetics and psychology, disciplines which no future critic can afford to ignore. He even implies that overtakes even the best of critics, like Dr. Johnson whose masterly *Lives of the Poets* we can now appreciate only by "an effort of historical imagination." Eliot writes : "Coleridge was perhaps the greatest of English critics, and in a sense the last." Eliot admires[35] Coleridge for the scope and variety of interests which he brings to bear on the discussion of poetry. The example of Coleridge to Eliot is a pointer to the fact that a literary critic when writing criticism should have wider studies and terms of reference, and literary criticism cannot remain wholly dissociated from other subjects.

Eliot takes Arthur Symons as a typical example of an "imperfect" and "impressionistic" critic, and illustrates his point by quoting from Symons :

> *Antony and Cleopatra is* the most wonderful, I think, of all Shakespeare's plays....The queen who ends the dynasty of the Ptolemias, has been the star of poets, a malign star shedding baleful light from Horace and Propertius down to Victor Hugo : and it is not to poets only....In her last days Claopatra touches a certain elevation....She would die a thousand times, rather than live to be a mockery and a scorn in men's mouths....She is woman to the last....So she dies....

It does not read like something from an essay on a work of art or a work of intellect. Symons here is living through the play and satisfying his suppressed wish and egotism. The difference between a perfect critic and Symons is that whereas the former, while trying to put his impressions into words, begins to analyse and reconstruct the work of art, the latter "begins to create something else."[36] Besides, the style of Symons is not essentially a prose style. It is much more like Swinburne's poetry.

Eliot believes that Swinburne as critic is better and more dependable than Symons. The language of Swinburn's criticism is not like a gilded, sentimental, purple patch. Swinburne does not fuse criticism with creation. His sensibility does not alter the object. His essay is by no means otiose and its stimulation is never misleading.

Swinburne's critical judgment is usually sound, temperate and just. His taste is sensitive and discriminating. Yet Swinburne is an appreciator and not a critic. There is a significant quality in Swinburne's criticism, which, as Eliot says, merits the attention of any good critic.

Eliot praises Dryden as critic and finds him far more disinterested and displaying free intelligence. Yet Dryden compared with Rochefoucauld is not quite a "free mind". In Dryden there is always a tendency to legislate rather than to inquire.

Eliot considers Johnson as one of the three greatest critics of poetry in English literature, the other two being Dryden and Coleridge. He presents Johnson as a typical example of "critical integrity."[37] For Johnson poetry was still poetry and not another thing. He is not usually led astray from the frontier of literary criticism. Eliot writes :

> Nineteenth century criticism, when it has not belonged primarily to the category of scholarly research, the presentation of the ascertainable facts about one author or another, has tended to be something less than purely literary. With Colersdge, criticism merges into philosophy and a theory of aesthetics; with Arnold it merges into ethics and propaedeutics, and literature becomes a means towards the formation of character; in some critics, of whom Pater is a specimen, the subject-matter of criticism becomes a pretext of another kind. In our own day.... influences of social disciplines have enlarged the field of the critic and have affirmed in a world which otherwise is inclined to depreciate the importance of literature, the relation of literature to life. But from another point of view this enrichment has also been an impoverishment, for the purely literary values, the appreciation of good writing for its own sake, have become submerged when literature is judged in the light of other considerations.[38]

If a critic is busy with the moral, religious and the other implications of a poem, poetry becomes a pretext for some kind of discourse. But there is no less danger on the other side. If one sticks too closely to the poetry and adopts no attitude towards what the poet has to say, one will evacuate it of all significance. Besides, there is a philosophic borderline which one must not transgress too far or too often, if one wishes to preserve one's standing as a critic. In these respects Johnson, within limitations, is one of the great critics. One cannot reject his criticism as he is a dangerous man to disagree with.

Eliot very aptly makes a capital distinction between a limited sensibility and a defective sensibility.[39] Within his proper limits Johnson is a sensitive as well as a judicial critic. He was bound by the limitations of his own age but he did not suffer from defective sensibility.

Johnson attached importance to edification, and this term has become an object of derision as our time has changed; our beliefs and society are not as corporate and settled as they were in Johnson's time. For Johnson's time edification meant that poetry should have serious value for the reader. We fail to see that it is merely the notion of edification that has changed. Johnson like a good critic is not dogmatic or technical. Eliot points out the limitations of a dogmatic or technical critic :

> The dogmatic critic who lays down a rule, who affirms a value, has left his labour incomplete....In matters of great importance the critic must not coerce, and he must not make judgments of worse and better. He must simply elucidate....And again, the purely technical critic — the critic that is who writes to expound some novelty or impart some lesson to practitioners of an art — can be called a critic only in a narrow sense....[40]

Eliot regards the *Biographia Literaria* of Coleridge, Wordsworth's preface to *Lyrical Ballads* and Keats's Letters and his comments on poetry as significant contributions to criticism. In Keats's utterances on poetry and art, Eliot finds the flash of genius. His letters are said to be "the most notable and the most important ever written by any English poet."[41] They have brilliance and profoundity. Eliot quotes a thought-provoking passage from Keats :

> In passing, however, I must say one thing that has pressed upon me lately, and increased my Humility and capability of submission....and that is this truth....Men of genius are great as certain ethereal chemicals operating on the Mass of neutral intellect but they have not any individuality, any determined character....I

would call the top and head of those who have a proper self Men of Power.[42]

This sort of remark, says Eliot, made by a man so young as was Keats, can only be called the result of genius.

One finds that Eliot recognises Arnold as a critic only half-heartedly. He has learnt from him; yet he is justly and sometimes unjustly critical of him. *The Sacred* Wood, being the title of an Eliot book, is, according to George Watson, a very suggestive metaphor.[43] The Wood, no doubt, is the sacred grove of Nemi as described by Sir James Frazer in the first chapter *of The Golden Bough*. Mr. Waston quotes the lines *of* Frazer :

> In the sacred grove there grew a certain tree round which at any time of the day, probably far into the night, a grim figure might be seen to prowl. In his hand he carried a drawn sword, and he kept peering warily about him as if at every instant he expected to be set upon by an enemy. He was a priest and murderer; and the man for whom he looked was sooner or later to murder him and hold the Priesthood in his stead. Such was the rule of the sanctuary. A candidate for the priesthood could only succeed to office by slaying the priest, and having slain him, he retained office till he was himself slain by a stronger or a craftier.

"This rule of succession by the sword" provides a key to Eliot's attitude to Arnold. Eliot in one sense is a "priest" and a "murderer".

In spite of being critical and slighting in tone towards Arnold, Eliot sees some positive points in him. Eliot's ideal of criticism as the disinterested endeavour to see the object as it is really, seems to have been inspired by Arnold. Eliot says :

> The phrases by which Arnold is best known may be inadequate, they may assemble more doubts than they dispel, but they usually have some meaning.

And further :

> In a society in which the arts were seriously studied, in which the art of writing was respected, Arnold might have become a critic.

Arnold is held to be in some respects the most satisfactory man of letters of his age and Eliot says that we cannot afford to neglect Arnold.[44] Dryden, Jolfnson and Aronld have performed their critical task as well as human frailty will allow. Each new master of criticism, Eliot says, performs a useful service merely by the fact that his errors are of a different kind from the last, and the longer the sequence of critics we have the greater the amount of correction possible. Eliot writes in praise of Arnold :

> But you cannot read his essay on the study of poetry without being convinced by the felicity of his quotations; to be able to quote as Aronld could is the best evidence. The essay is a classic in English criticism : so much is said in so little space with such economy and with such authority.[45]

In his essay, "To Criticise the Critic", Eliot writes about several types of critics and distinguishes them. First of all he does the professional critic. A professional critic is he whose literary criticism is the chief, perhaps his only title, to fame. Eliot terms the professional critic as the Super Reviewer, for he has often been the official critic for some magazine and newspaper, Eliot includes in this category Saint-Beuve, Paul Elmer More, Desmond MacCarthy, and Edmund Gosse. The professional critic may not be always like Saint-Beuve, a failed creative writer.

The second type of critic, Eliot points out, is the critic with gusto. This critic is not so much a judge as an advocate of the authors whose work he expounds, authors who are sometimes forgotten or unduly despised. He calls our attention to the merits of the writers — to whom we are indifferent — and helps us to see beauty and charm where we thought to be only boredom. George Saintsbury, Charles Whibley and Quiller-Couch belong to this type.

The third type of critic is the Academic and the Theoretical. W.P. Ker, I.A. Richards with his disciple William Empson, along with scholarly others, are of this type.

Eliot mentions Dr. F.R. Leavis as a "critic of importance" but he also calls him the "critic as moralist".

And finally Eliot comes to the critic whose criticism may be said to be a by-product of his creative activity. In this context,

Eliot mentions Samuel Johnson and Coleridge; Dryden and Racine in their prefaces; Matthew Arnold with reservation; and it is into this company that Eliot shyly intrudes.

Eliot declared in his dissertation that the aim of a critic should be to avoid pontificating formulae. The best criticism of Eliot is not tethered to a single prescribed rule. It displays more than one method or critical mode. Like any good critic Eliot defies his own prescribed rules. At his best, he combines in himself several approaches of literary criticism — the textual, biographical, sociological and humanistic. He employs different resources on different occasions for the adequate analysis of a poem and the full grasp of facts. He examines a case according to its nature and merit. He does not believe in any fixed, absolute critical method. Eliot says in "Tradition and the Individual Talent" that to divert interest from the poet to the poem is a laudable aim for a critic, yet he does not treat this as a laudable formula for examining every author and writer. In his practical criticism of some poets he does not sidetrack the personal, private or biographical factor. He says it is difficult, in considering Byron's poetry, not to be drawn into an analysis of the man. This kind of realisation on the part of Eliot is a pointer to the fact that he has range and flexibility as a critic. He is a classicist who extends his praise to a work of art for its depths of feeling. He appreciates Don *Juan for* "the genuine self-revelation" and "genuine emotion" :

> What puts the last cantos of *Don Juan* at the head of Byron's work is, I think, that the subject-matter gave him at least an adequate object for a genuine emotion. The emotion is hatred of hypocrisy; and if it was reinforced by more personal and petty feelings, the feelings of the man who as a boy had known the humiliation of shabby lodgings with an eccentric mother, who at fifteen had been clumsy and unattractive and unable to dance with Mary Chaworth....this mixture of the origin in his attitude towards English society only gives it greater intensity....It is difficult, in considering Byron's poetry, not to be drawn into an analysis of the man....[46]

Eliot examines George Herbert's poetry, not leaving out an

account of Herbert's family, hereditary influences, education and training. In his essay on Herbert he writes :

> The family background of a man of genius is always of interest. It is of interest to us because it was important to him. That two poet-brothers (George Herbert and Edward Herbert) should appear in a family so conspicuous for war-like deeds, administrative gifts and attendance at Court can only be accounted for by the fact that their mother was a woman of literary taste and of strong character and of exceptional gifts of mind as well as beauty and charm....If we remember Herbert's knowledge of music and his skill at the instrument, we appreciate all the better his mastery of lyrical verse.[47]

At one time Eliot spoke highly of the separation between "the man who suffers" and "the mind which creates", but in actual practice he appreciates a work of art also for its being "the record of spiritual struggles" and "emotional intensity". Eliot says *The Temple is* to be regarded not simply as a collection of poems but as a record of the spiritual struggles of intellectual power and emotional intensity who gave much toil to perfecting his *verses*. Eliot in "Shakespeare and the Stoicism of Sencea"[48] writes that the deep surges of Shakespeare's general cynicism and disillusionment are merely gigantic attempts to metamorphose private failures and disappointments.

The way Eliot approaches Wordsworth criticism in *The Use of Poetry* can be said to be sociological in the best sense of the term. Eliot writes that any radical change in poetic form is likely to be the symptom of some very much deeper change in society and the individual. Eliot makes the following reasonable and convincing statement :

> Nor am I indulging in sociological criticism which has to suppress so much of the data, and which is ignorant of so much of the rest. I only affirm that all human affairs are involved with each other, that consequently all history involves abstraction, and that in attempting to win a full understanding of the poetry of a period you are led to the consideration of subjects which at first sight appear to have little bearing upon poetry. These subjects have accordingly a good deal to do with the criticism of poetry....[49]

In another context Eliot writes that it is "impossible to fence off literary criticism from criticism on other grounds" :

> I have suggested also that it is impossible to fence off literary criticism from criticism on other grounds, and that moral, religious and social judgements cannot be wholly excluded....That they can, that literary merit can be estimated in complete isolation, is the illusion of those who believe that literary merit alone can justify the publication of a book which could otherwise be condemned on moral grounds.[50]

Eliot says no poet, no artist of any art has "his complete meaning alone". One must set him in contrast and comparison among the dead., Eliot means this is the principle of aesthetic and not merely historical criticism.

Eliot's essays on Dante, Marvell, Massinger, Swinburne, Ezra Pound, *In Memoriam,* Sir John Davies, and Dr. Johnson are among the best of his criticism, and in these essays one finds insight, explication, analysis and comparison, impersonality and objectivity, relevant intensity and generalization based upon textual examination.

In his essay on Dante, Eliot critically compares a passage of Dante with one from Shakespeare and shows their difference of function. Dante's line : "And sharpened their vision (knitted their brows) at us like an old tailor peering at the eye of his needle." And Shakespeare's line : "She looks like sleep/As she would catch another Antony/In her strong toil of grace".

Here the purpose of the type of simile of Dante, Eliot says, is solely to make us see more definitely the scene which Dante has put before us in the preceding lines, whereas the image of Shakespeare is much more complicated than Dante's; for "catch in toil" is a metaphor, and its purpose is to add to what we see, a reminder of that fascination of Cleopatra which shaped her history and that of the world, and of that fascination being so strong that it prevails even in death.

Even when Eliot steps out of the frontiers of literary criticism and insists on the primacy of the supernatural over the natural life, he is stimulating, "Pure" literature does not exist; it is, says Eliot, "a chimera of sensation" :

Even the purest literature is alimented from non-literary sources, and has non-literary consequences. Pure literature is a chimera of sensation : and admit the vestige of an idea and it is already transformed. We must include besides creative work and literary criticism any material which should be operative on general ideas.[51]

It is quite natural on the part of a human being to speculate on the ultimate meaning of human life and the universe and to tend to the ethical and the supernatural, for the objects of the world cannot be fully understood only in a temporal, secular light. In "Religion and Literature", Eliot says that the whole of modern literature is "corrupted" by what he calls secularism, that it is simply unaware of, simply cannot understand the meaning of, the primacy of "the supernatural over the natural life"; of something which Eliot assumes to be our primary concern. Eliot's essay, "Goethe as the Sage", is really a discourse in praise of wisdom. And be says in this essay that he can no longer confound the two wisdoms, as there is worldly wisdom and there is spiritual wisdom, and adds that Wisdom and Poetry are inseparable in the poets of the highest rank :

Literary criticism is an activity which must constantly define its own boundaries; also it must be going beyond them. The one invariable rule is, that when the literary critic exceeds his frontiers he should do so in full consciousness of what he is doing. We cannot get very far with Dante or Shakespeare or Goethe without touching upon theology and philosophy, and ethics and politics; and in the case of Goethe penetrating, in a clandestine way....into the forbidden territory of science.[52]

But the province of ethics is one from whose bourne very few literary critics return safely. And with the passage of years we see Eliot withdrawing from hand-to-hand fight with the fact, the absorbing attention to the word on the page, and struggling to make his peace with morality. In the preface to *After Strange Gods,* Eliot writes : "I ascend the platform of these lectures in the role of a moralist." It is no longer possible to say of Eliot what Eliot said of Blake : "Because he was not distracted or frightened or occupied in anything but, exact statements, he understood." Eliot is distracted by ethical generalizations, he wishes to consolidate, and his object is no longer to understand but to convert. His language now loses analytic nicety and masses itself to persuade, cajole and bludgeon.

The weakness of Eliot as a critic is manifest in his rare wilful distortion :

> Yet one cannot feel that a play like Congreve's. *Way of the World is* in some way more mature than any play of Shakespeare; but only in this respect, that it reflects a greater maturity of manners.

Dr. F.R. Leavis has rightly commented[53] on Eliot's statement : "What can maturity of manners' mean where manners are isolated in this way....What can maturity of manners be if not something to be discussed in terms of the relation between manners and more radical things (moral value should we say)."

Eliot's statement[54] that he fails to understand a stanza from Shelley's *Skylark* :

> Keen as are the arrows
> Of that silver sphere
> Whose intense lamp narrows
> In the white dawn clear
> Until we hardly see, we feel that it is there.

Does not seem very convincing, and his slight cannot altogether prejudice us against Shelley's poem.

Nobody realises better than Eliot the complexities of the critic's task. In his Foreword to Henri Fluchère's *Shakespeare,* Eliot lists several requirements for a complete Shakespearean critic :

> The ideal Shakespeare-critic should be a scholar, with knowledge not of Shakespeare in isolation but of Shakespeare in relation to the Elizabethan theatre, in relation to the social, political, economic and religious conditions of its time. He should also be a poet; and he should be a man of the theatre. And he should have a philosophic mind. Shakespeare's criticism cannot be written by a committee consisting of a number of specialized scholars, a dramatist, a producer, an actor,

a poet and a philosopher, each of them would be incompetent without sharing some of the knowledge and capacities of the other.[55]

In his Preface to *English Poetry and its Contributions to the Knowledge of a Creative Principle* by Leone Vivante, Eliot says that he has always remembered a distinction drawn by R.G. Collingwood at the beginning of *The Principle of Art*. Collingwood contrasts two types of theorists in the field of aesthetics: the "philosopher-aesthetician" and the "artist-aesthetician", and draws our attention to different types of errors to which they are exposed. Vivante, according to Eliot, seems to escape the mistakes of both.

The philosopher-aesthetician, as Eliot says, is frequently a philosopher who has thought it necessary, in order to complete his philosophical system, to produce a volume on aesthetics. The reason why he often fails to impress us, is because his theory appears to have no relation to our own appreciation of the arts; because he fails to deepen our understanding of the works of art which we do admire, to correct our taste when we like the wrong things and to open our minds to the enjoyment of other works of art to which we have been insensitive.

The artist-aesthetician, on the other hand, may rely too much upon his sensibility to compensate for his ignorance of philosophy and upon a solid foundation of experience he may erect a flimsy theory. He starts from those works of art which he admires.

That in the actual practice of criticism, Eliot sometimes goes against his own theory and formulation is the sign of a flexible and developing mind. A good critic at times turns down his own accepted formulae and does not lag behind in appreciating a new work of art.

REFERENCES

1. *Selected Essays*, p. 24.
2. *On Poetry and Poets*, p. 115.
3. *The Use of Poetry*, p. 180.
4. *To Criticise the Critic*, p. 20.
5. *The Sacred Wood*, p. 16.
6. *The Use of Poetry*, p. 21.

7. *To Criticise the Critic*, p. 11.
8. "Criticism in England", *Athenaeum*, 13 June 1919, p. 457.
9. *Selected Essays*, p. 32.
10. *Ibid.*
11. *Athenaeum*, May 1919.
12. Quoted by High Kenner, *The Invisible Poet T.S. Eliot*, London, W. Allen, 1960, p. 78.
13. *To Criticise the Critic*, p. 33.
14. *Selected Essays*, pp. 32, 326.
15. *Ibid.*, p. 29.
16. *Ibid.*, p. 27.
17. Ibid., p. 33.
18. *Ibid*, p. 25.
19. *Ibid.*, p. 30.
20. *On Poetry and Poeis*, p 112.
21. *Ibid*, p. 117.
22. Winehelesee, Rye and Denis Duval, *Scribner's Magazine*, XXIX (G. 1901, 45).
23. *On Poetry and Poets*, p. 114.
24. "Experiment in Criticism", included in *Literary Opinion in America*, Vol. 2, ed. by M. D. Zabel, New York, p. 616.
25. "Experiment in Criticism", an essay by Eliot.
26. *Ibid.*
27. *Ibid.*
28. *The Sacred Wood.*
29. *Ibid.*
30. *Ibid.*, p. 12.
31. *Ibid.*, p. 15.
32. *The Sacred Wood*, p. 31.
33. *The Use of Poetry*, p. 77.
34. *The Use of Poetry*, p. 79.
35. *On Poetry and Poets*, p. 134.
36. *The Sacred Wood*, p. 5.
37. *The Use of Poetry*, p. 64.
38. *On Poetry and Poets*, p. 121.
39. "Johnson as Critic and Poet", *One Poetry and Poets*, p. 166.
40. *The Sacred Wood*, pp. 11-12.
41. *The Use of Poetry*, p. 100.
42. *Ibid.*, p. 101.
43. *The Literary Critics*, p. 187
44. *The Use of Poetry*, p. 105.

45. *Ibid.*, p. 118.
46. *On Poetry and Poets*, p. 205.
47. T.S. Eliot, *George Herbert,* published for the British Council, 1962.
48. *Selected Essays*, p. 137.
49. *The Use of Poetry*, pp. 25-26.
50. *To Criticise the Critic*, pp. 25-26.
51. "The Idea of a Literary Review", *The Criterion*, No. 1, January, 1926.
52. *On Poetry and Poets*, p. 215.
53. F.R. Leavis, "Eliot's Stature as Critic", *Commentary,* XXVI, November 1958, p. 404.
54. *Dial,* 84 (March 1928, pp. 248-49).
55. Eliot's Foreword to *Shakepeare* by Henry Fluchére, London, 1953, pp. vi-vii.

5

The Dramatic Criticism

Eliot's dramatic criticism may be roughly divided into three parts — the theory of drama (specially the poetic drama), the critical analysis of individual dramatists, and Eliot's views and comments on his own dramatic experiments.

The essentially dramatic nature of Eliot's early verse has been sufficiently demonstrated in the criticism of F.R. Leavis and others. From the very beginning of his career Eliot aspired unconsciously for the theatre. Regarding his predilection towards drama Eliot writes :

> Reviewing my critical output for the last thirty odd years, I am surprised to find how constantly I have returned to the drama, whether by examining the work of the contemporaries of Shakespeare, or by reflecting on possibilities of the future.[1]

In drama too Eliot wants to bring a new turn by his theory and practice. Eliot wants verse drama, but the verse is to be spoken by characters or persons who use telephones, motor cars, and land on the moon. In short, the poetry of verse drama should be based upon the speech rhythms of contemporary situations and people, yet its task is not to picture the ephemeral, the superficial, the temporal and the external, but to peer beneath the surface, and to have a musical pattern. Eliot finds the justification of verse drama in the fact that verse or poetry is most natural to us in moments of emotional intensity. The aim of unlimited realism of prose dramatists like Jones, Gal sworthy, Pinero and Shaw does not impress him. Though Eliot himself had not full success in his own drama, yet his theory and experimentation are a pointer to a new direction. Eliot's theory of verse drama is a curb on the over-insistence on the realism of prose drama. A prose dramatist also can be poetic but he will after all have some limitation and will not have free play for the full exercise of his poetic sensibility. For drama a new verse but different from the blank verse of Shakespeare has to be forged. It has to be made transparent and flexible and hence capable of expressing any experience — the prosaic matters of today or the doleful songs of battles fought long ago. It means, as Eliot says, that poetry will not be "poetry" all the time and it need not be.

Eliot's critical analysis of dramas is different from that of A.C. Bradley, Charles Lamb, Swinburne and Coleridge. Inspired by Eliot, modern critics like L.C. Knights, D.A. Traversi and F.R. Leavis stress the imagery and the poetry of a play.

Great art is generally dramatic in the sense that it is objective, impersonal, intense, and it represents at the same time tremendous struggle and moral conflict. Every writer, whether novelist or poet, has dreamed of transporting his visions, his imagined characters on to the stage and submitting them to the glare of the footlights.

Eliot says that the epic is essentially a tale told to an audience, while drama is essentially an action exhibited to an audience.[2] We are human beings, and in what are we more interested than in human action and human attitudes?[3] Permanent literature," Eliot writes, "is always a representation: either a presentation of thought, or a presentation of feeling by a statement of events in human action or objects in the external world....The *Agamemnon* or *Macbeth* is equally a statement, but of actions."[4] Eliot opines : "The drama is perhaps the most permanent, is capable of greater variation and of expressing more varied types of society, than any other."[5]

In his essay "A Dialogue on Dramatic Poetry", Eliot refers to the link between the drama and the ceremony of the Mass. The origin of drama has really been from religious ritual, The ritual of the Church had something dramatic in it, and by the tenth century that ritual extended into the rudiments of a play. During the Easter celebrations, Biblical incidents like the visit of the three women to the empty tomb was sung by priests, with accompanying words chanted in Latin.

The desire for the dramatic is innate in human beings and constantly craves for fulfilment; such desire is existent even in those who attend the Mass with religious faith and seek gratification. Eliot writes :

> He went to High Mass every Sunday....His attention was not on the meaning of the Mass, for he was not a believer....it was on the art of the Mass. His dramatic desires were satisfied by the Mass precisely because he was not interested in the Mass, but in the drama of it....And even if you are a believer, you will have dramatic desires which crave fulfilment otherwise....We need (as I believe) religious faith. And we also need amusement A devout person, in sitting at Mass, is not in the frame of a person attending a drama, for he is participating — and that makes all the difference. In participating, we are supremely conscious of certain realities, and unconscious of others. But we are human beings, and crave representations in which we are conscious, and critical, of these other realities. We cannot be aware solely of divine realities. We must be aware also of human realities, And we crave some liturgy less divine, something in respect of which we shall be more spectators and less participants, Hence, we want the human drama, related with the divine drama, as well as the Mass.[6]

One of the important and major critical contentions of Eliot is that it is false to consider the drama merely as a part of literature. Literature is an art dependent upon words, but the drama is a multiple art, using words, scenic efforts, music, the gestures of the actors, and the organising talents of a producer. Some people have wrongly believed that a play can be made out of a series of finesounding speeches. A.C. Swinburne adhered to this heresy. Shakespeare knew that the play must come first, and the words, however brilliant, must be subservient to it. Charles Lamb has a typical Romantic attitude towards drama. He takes Shakespeare's tragedies, especially King Lear, as fine literature and says that they cannot be acted. He believes that King Lear, even after being properly and efficiently staged, cannot express to us the beauty and the fulness of its meaning which reading alone is supposed to do. That the bad and inadequate acting of a play can be jarring is understandable to us, but to consider King Lear too sublime and too fine to be acted is to fall prey to the typical subjectivism of the nineteenth century. Charles Lamb in his essay, "On the Tragedies of Shakespeare", mistakes acting for a buffoon's gesture or physical, jocular trick of the eye ear or hand, whereas in actuality good and proper acting brings the bidden, the incomprehensible currents and cross-currents of emotional experiences to clarity and intelligibility which reading alone cannot do.

G.B. Harrison writes[7] that one of the first points to be assumed by Aristotle, and yet so commonly overlooked, is that a drama is a "doing" or an "acting", and the "Shakespearean" play means that it was written for performance by a particular company of players in their own playhouse, catering to their own special audience. Eliot argues :

The play of King Lear can never be popular in a civilization so corrupted with literary culture that it resents what it cannot diminish. For there is a form of literary culture which shrinks from direct contact with a great work of art. In reading a play you can avoid this contact; you may talk about play or you may write about it, or you may read what has been written about it; but if you sit through a performance in a theatre, you cannot attend to anything but the play itself.[8]

H.E.G. Granville-Barker also in the beginning of his perface to King Lear quotes Lamb's view (Lear is essentially impossible to be represented on stage) only to confute it. And he writes that Shakespeare being a practical playwright meant Lear to be acted. A profounder indictment of the play's stageworthiness, Granville Barker adds, comes from A.C. Bradley's Lectures on Shakespearean Tragedy. To A.C. Bradley, King Lear seems Shakespeare's greatest achievement, but not his best play". A.C. Bradley writes :

The stage is the test of strictly dramatic quality and King Lear is too huge for the stage. It has scenes immensely effective in the theatre; three of them....lose in the theatre very little of the spell they have for imagination....but that which makes the peculiar greatness of Lear — the immense scope of the work; the mass and variety of intense experience; the interpenetration of sublime imagination, piercing pathos and humour; the vastness of the convulsion both of nature and of human passions....all this interferes with dramatic clearness even when the play is read, and in the theatre not only refuses to reveal itself through the sense but seems to be almost in contradiction with their reports.

H.Granville-Barker says that whatever Shakespeare has written has the implied promise that in the theatre it would gain. Eliot writes :

> What I Wish to do is to define and illustrate a point of view towards the Elizabethan drama, which is different from that of the nineteenth-century tradition....

> The accepted attitude towards Elizabethan drama was established on publication of Charles Lamb's *Specimens*. By publishing these selections, Lamb set in motion the enthusiasm for poetic drama which still persists, and at the same time encouraged the formation of a distinction which is, I believe, the ruin of modern drama—the distinction between drama and literature. For the *Specimens* made it possible to read the plays as poetry while neglecting their function on the stage. It is for this reason that all modern opinion of the Elizabethans seems to spring from Lamb, for all modern opinion rests upon the admission that poetry and drama are two separate things. The difference between the people who prefer Elizabethan drama, in spite of what they admit to be its dramatic defects, and the people who prefer modern drama, although acknowledging that it is never good poetry, is comparatively unimportant. For in either case, you are committed to the opinion that a play can be good literature but a bad play and that it may be a good play and bad literature — or else that it may be outside of literature together.

> On the one hand we have a Swinburne,representative of opinion that plays exist as literature, and on the other hand William Archer, who....maintains the view that a play need not be literature at all. No two critics of Elizabethan drama could appear to be more opposed than Swinburne and William Archer; yet their assumptions are fundamentally the same....[9]

To Eliot's mind the ideal medium for poetry, as well as the most direct means of social usefulness for poetry, is the theatre. The task of a poet is to preserve and restore the beauty of a language and also to help it develop, and the beauty of the developed language will influence the people, literate or illiterate, most directly through the theatre. And this is what Eliot means by the social function of poetry in its largest sense. The language developed and refined by the poet will affect the speech and the sensibility of the whole nation. Every poet likes to have some direct social utility. By this, Eliot does not mean that he should do the task of the theologian or the sociologist. He would like to be something of' a popular entertainer and be able to think his, own thoughts behind a tragic or a comic mask. He desires to convey the pleasures of poetry to a larger group of people. No honest poet, Eliot says, can ever feel quite sure of the permanent value of what he has written — that is why he longs to have at least the satisfaction of having a part to play in society as that of'the music-hall comedian.

Eliot's essay on Marie Lloyd is really an essay on the theatrical and dramatic aspect of her art. The death of Marie Lloyd strikes Eliot as an important event and a significant loss to the world of art. Marie Lloyd, Eliot says, was the greatest music-hall artist of her time in England :

> ....no other comedian succeeded as well in giving expression to the life of that audience, in raising it to a kind of art. It was, I think, this capacity for expressing the soul of the people that made Marie Lloyd unique....
> Marie Lloyd's art will, I hope, be discussed by more competent critics of the theatre than I....The working man who went to the music-hall and saw Marie Lloyd in the chorus was himself performing part of the act, he was engaged in that collaboration of the audience with the artist which is necessary in all art and most obviously in dramatic art.[10]

Eliot further points out that drama and melodrama or the theatrical should subsist together as the life of one is dependent upon the other. Melodrama is perennial, and the craving for it is perennial. The frontier of drama and melodrama is not to be sharply divided as no drama has ever been greatly and permanently successful without the melodramatic element.

"What is difference," asks Eliot, "between *The Frozen Deep* and *Oedipus the King*? It is the difference between coincidence, set without shame or pretence, and fate — which merges into character. It is not necessary for high drama that accident should be eliminated; you cannot formulate the proportion of accident that is permissible. But in great drama character is always felt to be — not more important than plot — but somehow integral with plot."[11]

Though Eliot feels that the ideal of the perfection of poetic drama is almost a mirage or an unattainable ideal, yet he is constantly fascinated by it. To be a verse dramatist — an ideal of Eliot — is really to achieve a difficult feat. The verse dramatist is required to be not only a dramatist but also to be a writer of verse who is supposed not to pour lyricism in a poem but to have the dramatic and the theatrical sense and sensibility also. To be a verse dramatist in the right sense of the term is more difficult than merely to be a dramatist or a poet. The right verse drama, as one may conclude from Eliot's statements in different essays, has to combine the utmost fringe of subjectivity in human consciousness with the greatest range of objectivity. And this ideal, one may think, is somewhat elusive for human attempt, for it needs a superb or rare genius for its fulfilment and realisation. The task of verse drama is not only to transmit the superficies of human life and the world but mainly to render and focus almost at the farthest frontier of human consciousness, and to communicate the incomprehensible. Eliot aims at equating the function of verse drama with the function of superb music. Shakespeare has been able to do this in some of his tragedies, specially in the balcony scene of *Romeo* and *Juliet*. Yet a verse dramatist cannot go very far in this direction as the complete emulation of music may bring the annihilation of meaning in art. An ideal verse drama, Eliot reiterates, should touch and reach the utmost confines of human consciousness :

> I should not like to close without attempting to set
> before you....the ideal to which poetic drama should
> strive. It is an unattainable ideal....It seems to me that

> beyond the nameable, classifiable, emotions and motives
> of our consciousness when directed towards action —
> the part of life which prose drama is wholly adequate
> to express — there is a fringe of indefinite extent, of
> feeling which we can only detect, so to speak, out of
> the corner of the eye and can never completely focus;
> of feeling which we are only aware in a kind of
> temporary detachment'from action....This peculiar range
> of sensibility can be expressed by dramatic poetry at
> its moments of greatest intensity. At such moments, we
> touch the border of those feelings which only music
> can express. We can never emulate music, because to
> arrive at the condition of music, would be the annihila.
> tion of poetry, and specially of dramatic poetry.[12]

A verse drama, as Eliot puts the matter, is not drama draped or dressed into poetry. Poetry or verse in drama is not an added embellishment or ornament or some superimposition; rather it is the constituent and functional part of• the drama. Eliot very convincingly points out that in intense emotion we tend to express ourselves in verse and the neurologists can explain why it is so; somehow emotion and rhythm are akin to each other. That is why poetry or verse is most natural to us in our moments of intensity. And poetry is the only medium for giving expression to the dark, the hidden, the unknown, and the inward reality.

Eliot's dialogue on dramatic poetry seems to have been modelled on John Dryden's essay on Dramatic Poesy. The essays by both critics are in the form of dialogue, and bring capital emphasis on verse drama. Eliot ends his essay with the memory of John Dryden — "And meanwhile let us drink another glass of port to the memory of John Dryden." Dryden in his essay on dramatic poesy justifies not only verse but rhymed verse in drama through Neander. Some of Eliot's points about verse drama are quite similar to those of Dryden.

Dryden closes his essay on dramatic poesy with positive reference to the fact that verse is the most suitable form for drama. Crites in this essay says that rhymed verse is essentially an artificial form of expression since, "no man without premeditation speaks in rhyme", and he supports his argument with Aristole's opinion, that tragedy is best written in verse nearest prose.

To this Neander replies that in scrious plays where the subjects and characters are great and the plot unmixed with mirth, rhyme is as natural and effectual as blank verse :

> The necessity of a rhyme never forces any but bad or lazy writers to say what they would not otherwise. It is true, there is both care and art required to write in verse....Rhyme might be made as natural as blank verse by the well placing of the words.[13]

Eliot wants the realisation of verse drama to the extent that in the words of Dryden it may leave "nothing in soul of the hearer to desire". We have this kind of supreme feeling when we are listening to a superb piece of music, and verse drama, according to Eliot, should arouse an effect in us almost like that of the "supernatural music from behind the wings". "The Function of Poetry in Drama" by Lascelles Abercrombie is very similar to Eliot's essay "Poetry and Drama".

He wrote this essay much before Eliot. He too is emphatic on the use of poetry as a medium of drama and holds verse drama to be superior to prose drama. By virtue of its verse rhythm, it is capable of transmitting to us the "spiritual reality" or the "emortional reality" of human life and the universe. He too says that a poetic play is not a play that might have been written in prose but happens to be written in poetry. He takes poetry rather than prose as the natural and straightforward medium for a play. According to him, in a perfectly successful verse play, talk of every level and kind can be done most naturally. A prose drama too can be poetic no doubt, but ideally speaking, it will be less poetic than a verse play which has the resources of rhyme, metre, music and metaphor. Abercrombie suggests the capitat function of drama, by using the word "intoxication". In poetry, the utterance has been fermented into metre and heady imagery. To use spoken poetry as the medium of drama is to obey' simply and without violence, the fundamental nature of drama. Prose drama is an "adulteration" for Abercrombie and a "by-product" for Eliot.

Abercrombie concludes enthusiastically : "I would labour for a movement to set going once more the drama which can most mightily intoxicate men to be consciously and diligently in love with life itself, yes, even with the tragedy of life.[14]

Eliot's essay, "Poetry and Drama", is an improvement on Abercrombie's essay "The Function of Poetry in Drama" in the sense that the former brings to us a modern and contemporary significance and deals with the excellence of poetry in terms of the dramatic. Eliot, unlike Abercrombie, reiterates in his essay that poetry in drama must iustify itself dramatically, that is, it must push the plot onwards and bring some direct or indirect light on the significance of the story or a particular character of the drama. And this task is more difficult in practice as it demands of a poet-dramatist the complete mastery of the theatrical sense. Abercrombie in his essay does not examine poetry in the light of the "dramatic". He does not insist on the pertinent, obvious fact that the aura or the magic of poetry has to have its breath only in the dramatic context. Only in this context can verse justify itself in drama. Eliot says that the finest poetry in Shakespcare's plays is also the most dramatic.

In his introduction to *Shakespéare and the Popular Dramatic Tradition* by S.L. Bethell, Eliot states :

A verse play is not a play done into verse but a different kind of play : in a way more realistic than naturalistic drama, because instead of clothing nature in poetry, it should remove the surface of things, expose the underneath, or the inside, of the natural surface appearance. It may use any device to show their real feelings and volitions, instead of just what, in actual life, they would normally profess or be conscious of; it must reveal underneath the vacillating or infirm character, the indomitable unconscious will; underneath the resolute purpose of the planning animal, the victim of the circumstance and the doomed or sacrificial being.[15]

Eliot's ideal of a verse-drama is that it should have a musical design and a musical pattern, and should have capability to arouse in us almost the same kind of intoxication, the aura, the ecstatic delight and the fulness which good music creates. A verse-drama should have a pattern behind a pattern, and should make us aware of it. It should have doubleness in action, as if happening at two planes at once. Eliot could not have the desired success in his own plays but what he says about the success and failure of the experimentation of his own versedrama is the most significant part of his dramatic criticism. In *Murder in the Cathedral* he could not solve the problem of language for his other verse plays or other versedramatists; in other words he could not forge a verse or idiom based upon the speech rhythms of the modern age. Though the chorus has some function in this play, Eliot likes it to be more integrated with the play. For a new verse-dramatist it is more easy to compose choral verse than to write actually dramatic lines.

In the verse of *The Family Reunion,* Eliot achieves the idiom of contemporary speech and thus is able to solve the problem of language. But Eliot's success in versification in this play is only at the cost of plot and character. Besides, the device of a lyrical duet used in two passages is further isolated from the rest of the dialogue. These passages are actually "beyond character". Eliot confesses that these passages, being simply poetic patches, are very much remote from the necessity of action. The passages are too much like "operatic arias". One who employs this sort of thing is putting up with a suspension of the action in order to enjoy a poetic fantasia.

Eliot in *The Cocktail Party* lays down for himself the ascetic rule to avoid poetry which cannot stand the test of strict dramatic utility. He believes that the selfeducation of a poet trying to write for the theatre seems to require a long period of disciplining his poetry, and putting it, so to speak, on a very thin diet in order to, adapt it to the needs of the stage :

> If the poetic drama is to reconquer its place as I have said, people are prepared to put up with verse from the lips of personages dressed in the fashion of some distant age; therefore, they should be made to hear it from people dressed like ourselves, living in houses and apartments like ours, and using telephones and motor-cars and radio-sets....What we have to do is to bring poetry in which the audience lives and to which it returns when it leaves the theatre; not to transport the audience into some imaginary world totally unlike its own....What might be achieved, by a generation of dramatists having the benefit of our experience, is that the audience should find at the moment of awareness that it is hearing poetry that it is saying to itself : "I could talk poetry too."[16]

In his essay "Three Voices of Poetry", Eliot looks more deeply into the subject of verse-drama and becomes more clear about it and brings to us useful points of distinction in art like the "dramatic", "quasi-dramatic" and the "non-dramatic". In the "three voices of poetry", the first is the voice of the poet talking, to himself and the second is the voice of the poet addressing an audience, whether large or small, while the third is the voice of the poet when he attempts to create a dramatic character speaking in verse, when he is saying, not what he would say in his own person, but only what he can say within limits of one imaginary character addressing another imaginary character.

Dramatic poetry is different from dramatic monologue. In a verse play, as Eliot says, the dramatist is not supposed to identify a character with himself and give him all the "poetry" to speak. The task of the verse-dramatist is more than that of a dramatic monologuist. He has, to distribute verse and also poetry to different characters according to their taste, temperament, education, intelligence, and background. Even if poetry is suitable to a character, the dramatist has to see that it forwards the action also. In this way we find that the verse dramatist has to work under dramatic checks and balances whereas the writer of the dramatic monologue has no such checks. A Browning may take the role of someone, some known historical or traditional figure, and may pour his liquid sentiment in a readymade mould or mask. The personage of the verse-drama on the stage must not give the impression of being merely the mouthpiece of the author. Hence, the dramatic monologue can be called "quasi-dramatic" and not fully dramatic.

Then there is closet-drama which should not be considered always as a term of reproach. This kind of drama was invented by Seneca and it had its influence on other kinds of drama. The study of closet-drama may be beneficial to us. It may cast further light on the dramatic problem. It is wrong on the part of a critic to treat Seneca's drama as a "bastard" form. Seneca surely created his own genre, and critics of drama are usually victims to narrowness while passing judgement on the dramatic or the undramatic; they do not have in their mind more than one or two kinds of drama. A critic can reach the right conclusion by having some knowledge of various forms of drama.

We can know "what is dramatic" much better, as Eliot says, if we are saturated in the Japanese Noh, in Bhasa and Kalidasa, in Aeschylus, Sophocles and Euripides, in Aristophanes as well as the great English and French drama. And Seneca's is definitely a form and his form is a practical form : it is even, Eliot suggests, a form which might be interesting to attempt in our own time, when the revival of the theatre is obstructed by some of the difficulties which made the stage an impossibility in the age of Seneca.

In a good verse-drama the dramatist is meant to have a point of view, some deeper meaning, some vision or some purpose to give animation and emotional depth to the play. In a good play, there should be general significance, an emotional depth (for the two go together), without which no action can be justified. The lack of this quality separates, as Eliot opines, the plays of John Ford from the best plays of Webster, Middleton and Tourneur. He holds that the characters of a play should dramatise, though in no obvious form, the drama and struggle of life. There should be transfusion of personality into the impersonal work of art otherwise the characters would turn out to be "lubricious prudes"[17] A living character is not necessrily "true to life". What the creator of character needs is not so much knowledge of motives as "keen sensibility". A character is not composed of scattered observations of human nature, but of the points which are felt together. A character, to be living, must be conceived from some emotional unity. Briefly, a versedrama must have "inner significance" and "symbolic value".

Sidney in his essay ridicules the play which does not cohere the comical and the tragic parts in the unity of feeling. Eliot justifies Sidney's point and says that Sidney is perfectly right.

The violence of contrast between the tragic and the comic, the sublime and the bathetic, disappears in the maturing work of Shakespeare. Eliot terms this "unity of feeling," also as "unity of sentiment". In his essay on Ben Jonson he calls it "unity of inspiration" which radiates into the plot and personages alike. Eliot takes this "unity of feeling" or "unity of sentiment" to be more important than the other laws of place and time. Eliot is not orthodox like Sidney regarding the laws of place and time. Sidney says "the stage should represent but one place, the utmost time presupposed in it should be, both by Aristotle's precept and common reason, but one day". This unity of place and time, Eliot says, "has worn out now. Eliot feels that the dramatic laws of the unities may sometimes be violated in order to gain something more, specially when the more important law, unity of feeling, is not disturbed. In poetry, as in life, our business is to make the best of a bad job. One can violate the law of unity of place if we preserve the law of unity of time, or *vice versa,* or we may violate both when we observe more closely the law of unity of feeling. Eliot takes unity of sentiment to be a larger and more important term than unity of action.

The essay on *Hamlet* represents the typical trend of Eliot's dramatic criticism. The way of Eliot's criticism of drama is to consider the whole rather than the part, the pattern and a developing personality that constantly emerge from the whole sequence of the plays of a playwright. To know the best in Shakespeare or in any other dramatist one should read all his plays. This insistence on the whole rather than the part is F.H. Bradleyan rather than A.C. Bradleyan in temper.

Eliot writes in *The Use of Poetry* :

> I am not every much interested in deciding which play of Shakespeare is greater than which other; because I am more and more interested, not in one play or another, but in Shakespeare's work as a whole....but if any one of Shakespeare's plays were omitted we should not be able to understand the rest as well as we do.. In such plays we must consider not only the degree of unification of all the elements into a unity of sentiment, but the quality and kind of emotion to be unified and the elaborateness of the pattern of unification.[18]

A Bradleyite critic "hypostasizes" character and plot; Eliot insists on the pattern, or what we may call the inner significance which gradually emerges from the whole work of a dramatist. It was first of all Henry James who gave currency to the word "pattern". The pattern to be found in the works of Shakespeare,

Eliot says, is elaborate, complex, and inscrutable. In a lesser degree, this is to be found also in other dramatists like Ben Jonson, Marlowe, Webster and Chapman. The works of John Ford and Shirley obviously miss it. This pattern in drama is possible only when there is the "reality of moral synthesis" or a vision to inform the verse and a personality to give indefinable unity to the most various material. Eliot writes about Thomas Heywood :

> Behind the motions of his personages, the shadows of the human world, there is no reality of moral synthesis; to inform the verse there is no vision, none of the artist's power to give undefinable unity to the most various material. In the work of nearly all of those of his contemporaries who are as well known as he, there is at least some incohate pattern; there is....personality.[19]

Eliot appreciates Professor Wilson Knight's approach to Shakespeare in his introduction to *The Wheel of Fire*. He has not forgotten that a good play is primarily to be acted rather than to be read in privacy. He calls the plays of Shakespeare "an extended metaphor". He insists on the complexity, the richness, the design and the sequence of imagery in a play. He takes note of the "subterrene or submarine music" and makes a search for the pattern below the level of plot and character.

But I confess that reading his (Professor Wilson Knight's) essays seems to me to have enlarged my understanding of the Shakespeare pattern which after all is quite the main thing.

> To take the Shakespeare work as a whole, no longer to single out several plays as the greatest, and make the others only as apprenticeship or decline — is, I think, an important and positive step in modern Shakespeare interpretation. More particularly, I think that Mr. Wilson Knight has shown insight in pursuing his search for the pattern below the level of plot and character....
>
> Our first duty, as either critics or interpreters, surely must be to try to grasp the whole design, and read character and plot in the understanding of his subterrene or submarine music. Here I say Mr. Knight has pursued the right line for his own plane of investigation, not hypostasizing character and plot.[20]

Eliot has written little about Shakespeare but his critical methods and example have inspired others on the same line. The numerous essays on Shakespeare which have appeared in *Scrutiny* by James Smith, J.C. Maxwell, L.C. Knights, D.A. Traversi and F.R. Leavis together form a substantial body of criticism, starting always from the text and working outwards to an interpretation of the whole play.

Fashions in criticism change almost as completely as fashions in costume. Few modern critics have Bradley's point of vision. He was a philosopher, a moralist. He regarded Shakespeare's tragedies "as....a glimpse of the great problem of Good and Evil."

Eliot has more praise for a critic like H. Granville-Barker. In his prefaces to Shakespeare, he illuminates the plays with the understanding of the producer and suggests the need for a synthesis of the several points of view from which Shakespeare can be studied.

Eilot's criticism of *Hamlet*, the play, is simple : the play, he, says, is an "artistic failure", because the dramatist here has not been able to achieve "unity of impression". The emotional utterances of Hamlet, the character, are in excess of the facts as they appear in the play. The excessive emotion in Hamlet is not contained in the situation or explained by the situation as given in the play. Hence, the play has failed to achieve a pattern. Shakespeare has not been able to objectify his obscure emotions in the play. The play lacks in, "artistic inevitability" or the complete adequacy of the external to the emotion. The terrible, intense feeling in the play is without an object or is exceeding its object. This is not the case with the more successful tragedies of Shakespeare. The principle of "objective correlative", though mostly true for drama, is also true, to a great extent, for other forms of art in general. A.E. Housman in a poem denounces God as a "blackguard" and "brute" just because the poet's walking in the evening has been spoiled due to rain. The denunciation of Housman does not have artistic inevitability; rather it looks trifling. The powerful, passionate questionings and interrogation of Job to God have complete adequacy of the external. They are fully intelligible in the situation and are never jarring. The excessive emotion or passion in the Book of Job as well as *The Brothers*

Karamazov is wholly contained in the situation and we do not
feel in these books that there is merely the showman's show as
in the case with A.E. Housman.

The emotional intensity in *King Lear* issues overwhelmingly
and most naturally from the context of the play. Eliot defines his
notion of the "objective correlative."

> The only way of expressing emotion in the form of art
> is by finding an objective correlative : in other words
> a set of objects, a situation, a chain of events which
> shall be the formulae of that particular emotion; such
> that when the external facts, which must terminate in
> sensory experience, are given, the emotion is
> immediately evoked. If you examine any of Shakespeare's
> more successful tragedies, you will find this exact
> equivalence; you will find that the state of mind of
> Lady Macbeth walking in her sleep has been
> communicated to you by a skilful accumulation of
> imagined sensory impressions.[21]

Hamlet, the character, is not only out of tune with the central
theme of lust and betrayal but is rather groping at something
different and at quite a different experience. One finds that Hamlet
is trying to understand the Mystery and terror of a man's life
after death. In Hamlet's utterances one detects the fusion of
Shakespeare, the man, with Hamlet, the character. A human being
may not hold a belief that there is something positive after death;
hence, his inquiring mind may be groping to know the mystery
after death. As he cannot be certain about the unknowable (*i.e.*,
the region of death) he is struck with awe, terror, mystery, and
despair at the nothingness of human existence. This seems to be
the attitude of Hamlet with which Shakespeare the man seems to
be identifying.

But this attitude has no justification in the play. "What is
man but the quintessence of dust" seems to be the genuine
experience of Hamlet, but it is not at all relevant to the central
theme (the theme of lust and betrayal) which had begun at the
beginning.

Eliot's stricture on Hamlet does not mention the lines which
do not have this relevance or equivalence. Some critics are not

at all convinced by Eliot's view regarding Hamlet. H.B. Charlton in his introduction to Shakespearian Tragedy writes :

> When, for instance, I read that *Hamlet* "so far from being Shakespeare's masterprise....is certainly an artistic failure", I feel that English is a language which I do not know.[22]

David L. Stevenson, too, in an article[23] says that Eliot in his essay reaches an oddly arbitrary conclusion. J. Dover Wilson, in an appendix to his detailed study *What Happens in Hamlet* (1935), patiently disagrees with Eliot. Francis Furgusson in his *The Idea of Theatre* regards Eliot's essay as an outstanding example of a perverse demand for narrow conceptual truth from a play intricately dramatising the mystery of life itself. A writer of the stature of André Gide, in an interview with Philip Roddman (as reported in *Partisan Review,* February 1949) refuses to discuss Eliot's analysis of the play at all. Delmore Schwartz says : "To conclude that *Hamlet is* failure, as Eliot does....seems to me to have a curious notion of success."

Eliot's criticism of the Elizabethan dramatists is a considerable part of his dramatic criticism. The essays constitute a genuine revaluation of some of these dramatists. His task has been also to bring them into a new focus. Revaluation is no less a critical function; it requires great fortitude, courage, and agility of mind. Eliot's revaluation has influenced the courses of studies and the prescription of books in universities.

Ben Jonson was taken as a liability in the balancesheet of English literature though his learning and scholarship were granted by the earlier critics. The reputation of Ben Jonson in the past was of the "deadly" kind. Ben Jonson seemed to arouse in the reader no creative curiosity. The credit goes to Eliot that he has revalued Ben Jonson and shown by textual analysis that he is genuinely creative and delightful, and is possessed of a vision of life. Though the characters of Ben Jonson are not three-dimensional like those of Shakespeare, they are infused with definite animation, verve and individuality. They cannot be accounted only in terms of the theory of Humours. If fiction is classed into creative and critical fiction, Ben Jonson's drama, says Eliot, will belong to the creative.

Eliot has brought neglected and less known figures, like Thomas Middleton, Thomas Heywood, Cyril T'ourneur, John Ford and John Marston into better focus. Eliot has looked into the work of these Elizabethan dramatists not merely from the viewpoint of craftsmanship. His approach to them is not that of a naive, narrow and dry classicist. While writing his critical analysis of the Elizabethan dramatists, Eliot insists on the point of personality, a pattern or viewpoint, some unifying purpose and emotional unity, and asserts that a play cannot have its real life without them. Philip Massinger, for example, utilises convention, but convention in the work of Massinger, says Eliot, remains convention and nothing more. Convention or a particular belief of a particular generation is only an alloy for a dramatist, as for any other artist, and he has to mix it with his gold, i.e., his own emotion and feeling and personal observation, And intellect needs to be at the tips of the senses. Eliot says that Massinger has not the sensitive nerves or keen sensibility or enough of his own personality to infuse life into the "alloy" or "convention" used by him. Shakespeare in his plays utilizes the convention of his age but supersedes it by virtue of his personality and imaginative power. His use of superstition and the supernatural is for satisfying the groundlings as well as for rendering the character's inward passions and desires and mental processes in crucial moments. Massinger's feeling for language, Eliot says, has outstripped his feelings for things. In Massinger's work, sensation does not become word, nor word sensation. Massinger deals not with emotions so much as with the social abstractions of emotions more generalised. And this is the chief deficiency in him. Eliot writes :

> The defect is precisely a defect of personality. He is not, however, the only man of letters who, at the moment when a new view of life is wanted, has looked at life through the eyes of his predecessors; and only at manners through his own.[24]

There should be the "transfusion of personality" into a work of art, which is wanting in Massinger's plays. Massinger and Fletcher alike, says Eliot, are not able to create "vivified", "passionate", complete human characters. A character to be living must be conceived from some emotional unity. Massinger inherits "traditions of conduct, female chastity, hymened sanctity, fashion of honour", without either criticizing or informing them from his own experience.

Eliot finds almost the same defect of "personality" or the lack of "personality" in the work of John Ford. The plays of John Ford do not have general significance and emotional depth (for the two go together) without which no action can be justified. From this angle we are convinced of the incommensurability of writers like Ford and Beaumont and Fletcher with Shakespeare. In their work there is no symbolic value, no unifying felt experience, little pattern or undertone of personal emotion, no personal drama of struggle. In short, John Ford's work has not the "inner significance" which Shakespeare's has. Eliot writes :

> Ford's poetry as well as Beaumont's and Fletcher's, is of the surface: that is to say, it is the result of the stock of expression of feeling accumulated by the greater men. It is the absence of purpose — if we may use the word "purpose" for something more profound than any formulable purpose can be — in such dramatists as Ford, Beaumont, Fletcher, Shirley and Otway....[25]

Unlike Massinger and John Ford, Middleton in his work has much of the inner truth and personality. He uses the convention but supersedes it by virtue of his observation and feeling. In his work there is a substratum of truth permanent in nature. *The Changeling*, Eliot says, is eternal tragedy. It is as permanent as *Oedipus* or *Antony* and *Cleopatra*. It is the tragedy of the not naturally bad but irrespossible and undeveloped nature caught in the consequences of its own action. It presents a dispassionate exposure of fundamental passions of any time and any place. Eliot writes about Middleton :

> The man (Middleton)....remains inscrutable, solitary, unadmired; welcoming collaboration, indifferent to fame....Yet he wrote one tragedy which more than the any play except those of Shakespeare has a profound and a permanent value and horror....[26]

Thomas Heywood, one of the dimmest figures, is brought to light by Eliot. The sensibility in him, says Eliot, is merely that of ordinary people in ordinary life. Behind the motions of Heywood's personages there is no reality of moral synthesis, and to inform the verse there is no vision. Yet Eliot finds in Heywood's work some positive points. He says the verse of *A Woman Killed with Kindness*, though nowhere bursting into a flame of poetry, is yet economical and tidy, and extracts all the dramatic value possible from the situation.

Eliot takes up the task of revaluing John Marston too, who, for both scholars and critic, has remained a territory of unexplored riches and risks, Eliot finds in John Marston the doubleness of reality, a "sense of something behind", a "pattern behind the pattern", and asserts that the aim of a poet dramatist is the presentation of this inner pattern and doubleness of action. Eliot writes :

> It is not by writing quotable "Poetic" passages, but by giving us the sense of something behind, more real than any of his personages and their action, that Marston established himself among the writers of genius.[27]

> In spite of the tumultuousness of the action, and the ferocity and horror of certain parts of the play, there is underlying serenity; and as we familiarize ourselves with the play, we perceive a pattern behind the pattern into which the characters deliberately involve themselves; the kind of pattern which we perceive in our lives only at rare moments of inattention and detachment, drowsing in sunlight. It is the pattern drawn by what the ancient world called Fate; subtilized by Christianity into mazes of delicate theology; and reduced again by the modern world into crudities of psychological or economic necessity.[28]

Tourneur, says Eliot, excels in three virtues of the dramatist : he knew, in his own way, bow to construct a plot, he was cunning in the manipulation of stage-effects, and he was a master of versification and choice of language.

Eliot says that *The Revenger's Tragedy* of Tourneur lacks the objective correlative. But in his essays concerning Tourneur, he does not mention the term. He says that *The Revenger's Tragedy* can be compared to *Hamlet*. The horrible vision of life has not been made integral with the drama. This kind of experience does not convince us as it is neither contained in the situation nor explained by it. Hence, the "cynicism, the loathing and disgust of humanity" expressed in *The Revenger's Tragedy* seem to be "prior to experience" or "the fruit of but little." They are immature in the respect that they "exceed the object." They are "static". An artist is required to compose his art with greater depth of feeling and intensity, with greater consistency and with a somewhat objective attitude, for the mature and convincing expression of disgust and hatred of life, suffering, cynicism and despair. The horrible vision of life, though consummately expressed in The *Revenger's Tragedy*, seems to us "adolescent, fragmentary, or the result of, few or slender experiences". In the novels of Hardy, the portrayal of the sufferings of human bgings often appears to us mature and convincing. This sense of consistency and objectivity is not wanting in Swift's expression of hatred and disgust. Eliot's comment on *The Revenger's Tragedy* admirably explains the nature of the play....

> It (*The Revenger's Tragedy*) does express. an intense, unique and horrible vision of life; but is such a vision as might come, as the result of few or slender experiences, to a highly sensitive adolescent with a gift for words....The cynicism, the loathing and disgust of bumanity, expressed consummately in *The Revenger's Tragedy*, are immature in the respect that they exceed the object... They might be prior to experience or be the fruit of but little; Swift's is the progressive cynicism of the mature and disappointed man of the world. As an objective comment of the world, Swift's is by far the more terrible....[29]

The term "Cobjcctive correlative" shows a classicist's concern in the good sense of the term. This term is new in its phrasing, though its content is age-old. It denotes essentially a quest for poise and balance in the realm of art. It is valid for every form of art but it is more relevant within drama. In a short lyric, a poet may simply express his emotions and impressions directly, without substantiating them, yet his poem may be a success. But a good dramatist cannot afford to work like that. A dramatist has to build up a series of events, situations, a framework or a scaffold of story, to make the emotional utterances seem inevitable. Lear's suffering, his ravings and intense feelinge are not irrelevant, as they are fully contained in the situation and explained by it. In the absence of the objective equivalent, the intensity of emotion in a drama will appear to us cheap, fake, sentimental, morbid, irrelevant and ineffective. The term "objective correlative" expresses the most common but the most fundamental and the universal necessity of art. By insisting on this necessity, Eliot has done a service to the world of literature and criticism. The objective correlative is not mentioned by its name but is discussed at many places in Eliot's work. For instance, in his essay on Lancelot Andrewes also, Eliot expresses the content of this term :

> Andrewes' emotion is purely contemplative, it is not personal, it is wholly evoked by the object of contemplation, to which it is adequate; his emotions wholly contained in and explained by its object....[30]

REFERENCES

1. "Poetry and Drama," *On Poetry and Poets*, p. 72.

2. "Three Voices of Poetry", *On Poetry and Poets*, p. 96.

3. "A Dialogue on Dramatic Poetry", *Selected Essays*, p. 51.

4. *The Sacred Wood*, p. 65.

5. The Possibility of a Poetic Drama," *The Sacred Wood*.

6. *Selected Essays*, p. 48.

7. G.B. Harrison, *Shakespeare's Tragedies* (Routleldge, 1963). p. 15.

8. *The Criterion*, April 1924, Vol. 11, No. 7, p. 235.

9. "Four Elizabethan Dramatists", *Selected Essays*, pp. 457-58.

10. "Marie Lloyd", *Selected Essays*, pp. 457-58.

11. *Ibid.*, p. 467.

12. *On Poetry and Poets*, p. 87.

13. "An Essay on Dramatic Poesy," *English Critical Texts*, ed. by D.J. Enright, Ernest De Chickera, p. 109.

14. The Function of Poetry in Drama", *English Critical Essays* (20th Century, first series), World Classics, p. 272.

15. Eliot's Introduction, *Shakespeare and the Popular Dramatic Tradition by* S.L. Bethel.

16. *On Poetry and Poets*, p. 82.

17. *Selected Essays*, p. 213.

18. *The Use of Poetry*, p. 44.

19. Selected Essays, p. 179.
20. Eliot's Introduction, *The Wheel of Fire*, 1954, pp. 18-19.
21. *The Sacred Wood*, p. 101.
22. H.B. *Charlton, Shakespearian Tragedies*, Cambridge University Press, 1961, p. 2.
23. *The Journal of Aesthetics and Art Criticism*, Vol. XIII, Sept. 1954, No. 1, p. 69.
24. *Selected Essays*, p. 220.
25. *Ibid.*, p. 204.
26. *Ibid.*, pp. 169-70.
27. *Ibid.*, p. 230.
28. *Ibid.*, p. 232.
29. *Ibid.*, pp. 189-90.
30. *Ibid.*, p. 34.

6
Criticism of the Novel

Eliot's criticism of novels needs a separate section for a detailed discussion. It has not been systematically explored, partly for the reason that Eliot himself speaks embarrassedly of his ability to write criticism of novels and further informs us that he is not a novel-reader. Except for one or two essays ("Wilkie Collins and Dickens" in *Selected Essays* and two essays on Henry James included in *The Question of Henry James*, edited by F.W. Dupee, and some pages on D.H. Lawrence and Thomas Hardy in *After Strange Gods*), almost all the Criticism of different novels and novelists remains uncollected and is buried in journals and periodicals like *The Athenaeum, The Dial, Horizon and The Hudson Review*. It is to be noted further that Eliot's criticism of novels is mostly in the form of reviews. But this fact does not diminish the importance of these reviews as criticism and we know that some of the brilliant critical essays in *Selected Essays, the Sacred Wood and on Poetry and Poets* were originally reviews.

Eliot has reviewed major novelists — English, French, American and Russian. He has dwelt upon Henry James, Hawthorne, Mark Twain, James Joyce, Wyndham Lewis, Collins and Dickens, Beyle and Balzac, Dostoevsky and Turgenev, Virginia Woolf, Lawrence and Hardy. In addition, Eliot has incidentally commented on Joseph Conrad and Flaubert too. From Eliot's likes and dislikes, praise and appreciation, some unifying principles about the requisites of the novel do emerge. Dr. Leavis's charge that "Eliot has never shown any intelligence about prose fiction"[1] does not seem quite fair.

What Eliot finds in the analysis of various novels is of permanent importance and of general interest to us. In his essays on Henry James, he insists on the pattern in the novel as well as on the integrity of the artist and the presentation of his vision. In Hawthorne, he finds firmness, the true coldness, the hard coldness of the genuine artist. He regards *Ulysses* as the most important expression which the present age has found. This book is, he seriously believes, a step towards making the modern world possible for art. Eliot finds in *Ulysses* the mythical method instead of the narrative method which is useful and suggestive for Eliot's own poetry and for the artist of the twentieth century in general. In Balzac, Eliot says, the fantastic element is of another sort; it is not an extension of reality, it is an atmosphere thrown upon reality direct from the personality of the writer. And Stendhal and Dostoevsky are superior to Balzac in the sense that they "strip the world". Stendhal's scenes and some of his phrases have the sharpness· of a razor's edge, like cutting one's own throat. The atmosphere of Balzac is the highest possible development of the atmosphere of Mrs. Radcliffe. Eliot says that Mark Twain, at least in *Huckleberry Funn*, has discovered a new way of writing, valid not for only himself but for others. He places him, in this respect, with Dryden and Swift, as one of those writers who have brought their language up-to-date and have "purified the dialect of the tribe." In the work of Mr. Lewis, he finds the thought of the modern and the energy of the cave man. Besides eccentricity of thought and feeling, sexual morbidity, lack of social and religious training, Eliot finds in D.H. Lawrence an insensibility to ordinary social morality. Thomas Hardy, to Eliot, is a case of extreme emotionalism, a symptom of decadence, and an interesting example of a personality uncurbed by any institutional attachment. Turgenev used Russian material naturally, with the simplicity of a genius turning to what his feelings knew best. In the obituary on Virginia Woolf, Eliot points out "the imaginative genius and the sense of style", her qualities of personal charm and distinction, of kindliness and wit, and of curiosity about human beings.

Eliot's points of praise regarding Henry James are of central significance for serious readers of the novel. Eliot points out that great novelists and poets have a pattern in their art. He has obviously been influenced by James, as the word "pattern" given currency by James himself recurs in Eliot's critical work. "Pattern" in a novel stands for beauty, unity, point of view, consistency, and a developing, maturing personality in the novelist. Eliot writes :

> The other part of the pattern is to be found in the work of....some of the greatest novelists, certainly of George Eliot, and of Henry James....[2]

While introducing *The Wheel of Fire*, Eliot says that the greatest prose like the greatest poetry has a doubleness, and considers Henry James "no less genuine a patternmaker than Dante."[3] Eliot's reviews of novels and novelists are usually general interpretation rather than detailed, proper criticism. Alan Holder writers in an article[4] that readers are struck by the frequency with which the name of Henry James gets into Eliot's criticism. In "Lettre d' Angleterre" (1923) in *La Nouvelle Révue Francaise*, Eliot names F. H. Bradley, Henry James and Sir James Frazer as his "masters". Eliot once called Henry James "the most intelligent man of his generation".

To insist on the pattern in a novel is to insist on the structural and textural design of it. In other words, it emphasises the fact that a novel is a tissue or a living organism, in which characters, dialogue, story, rhythm or action are simply constituents of or contributory to the pattern or the unity of impression. The ideal of pattern in a novel points to the aesthetic beauty, the artistic perfection, the wholeness, completeness and roundness of art. E.M. Forster dwells upon pattern :

> We can say only (so far) that pattern is an aesthetic aspect on the novel....it draws most of its nourishment from the plot....It springs mainly from the plot, accompanies it like a light in the clouds. Beauty is sometimes the shape of the book as a whole, the unity and our examination would be easier if it was always this....[5]

And later

> The longer James worked the more convinced he grew that a novel should be a whole — not necessarily geometric like *The Ambassadors*, but it should accrete

round a single topic, situation, gesture, which should
occupy the characters and provide a plot, and should
also fasten upon the novel on the outside, catch its
scattered statements in a net, make them cohere....A
pattern must emerge and anything that emerges not from
the pattern must be pruned off as wanton distraction....[6]

Eliot says[7] that the general scheme in the work of Henry James
is not of one character or a group of characters in a plot or merely
in a crowd. The focus is situation, a relation, an atmosphere, to
which the characters pay tribute, but being allowed to give only
what the writer wants. Eliot adds that, with character, in the sense
in which the portrayal of character is usually expected in the
English novel James had no concern. Had James been a better
hand at character, he would have been a coarser hand altogether
and would have missed the sensibility to create the peculiar data
of impression. Eliot notes that the books of Henry James form a
complete whole. One must read all of them, for one must grasp, if
anything, both the unity and the progression, the gradual
development and the identity of spirit. Professor L.C. Knights too
in his preface to *Explorations* writes about "the figure in the
carpet" of James's work. A critic's concern with the character of
a novel is a more limited concern than that with the pattern. To
stress, in a conventional way, character or plot or any of the other
abstractions that can be made, is to deny and neglect the total
response.

L.C. Knights in his essay "How Many Children had Lady
Macbeth" says[8] that the assumption that it is the main business
of a writer other than the lyric poet to create characters is not,
of course, confined to criticism of Shakespeare : it long ago
invaded criticism of the novel. He continues in the same essay
that the mass of Shakespeare criticism does not give a hint that
character — like plot, rhythm, construction and all our other
critical counters — is merely an abstraction from, the total
response in the mind of the reader or spectator brought into being
by written or spoken words. And this applies equally to the novel
or any form of art that uses language as its medium Dr. C.H.
Rickwood, in "A Note on Fiction", writes admirably regarding
the novel :

The form of novel only exists as a balance of response on the part of the reader. Hence, schematic plot is a construction of the reader's that corresponds to an aspect of the response and stands in merely diagrammatic relation to the source. Only as precipitates from the memory are plot or character tangible....[9]

Walter Allen in his introduction to *The English Novel*[10] says that a novel is a totality and of this totality characterization is only a part; yet it is plainly an essential one and the first in order of importance. Without it the most profound apprehensions of man's fate count for nothing. Only through character, Allen adds, can the novelist's apprehension of man's fate be uttered at all.

We have the impression from Eliot's essays[11] on Henry James that a novel is great not only by the beauty and perfection of its style but by the possession and communication of an ideal, a point of view or a vision. Eliot finds behind the greatness of Henry James's novels the imperative insistence of an ideal, a vision of an ideal society. He repudiates those who accord every praise to James's technique only :

> James has suffered the usual fate of those who, in England, have outspokenly insisted on the importance of technique. He has received the kind of praise usually accorded to some useless, ugly and ingenious piece of carving which has taken a very long time to make.[12]

> The example which Henry James offered us was not that of a style to imitate, but of an integrity so great, a vision so exacting that it was forced to the extreme of care and punctiliousness for exact expressions.[13]

That James's view of England, says Eliot, was romantic, is a small matter. James's romanticism implied no defect in observation of the things that he wanted to observe. It was not the romanticism of those who dream because they are too lazy or too fearful to face the facts; it issues rather from the imperative insistence of an ideal which tormented him. And yet, as Eliot says, no one in the end, has been more aware of the disparity between a possibility and a fact. James's last unfinished novels (*The Sense of the Post and The Ivory Tower*), at least, can hardly fail to prove this.

Some of Eliot's points of praise for Henry James are equally true of great art in general. A mastery over and an escape from "Ideas", Eliot says, are "perhaps the last test of a surperior intelligence". Eliot finds this quality in Henry James. James was a critic who "preyed not upon Ideas", but upon living beings. James did not provide us with "Ideas", but with another world of thought and feeling. The sharper intelligence or the finer sensibility of a great artist like the Shakespeare of Lear has no prepossessions; it simply explores the utmost extent of human possibility, the region of "nothingness", the no man's-land. It fears nothing, it blinkers nothing; it brings to us the fact, however terrible it is.

Eliot praises Henry James for this escape from "Ideas"; by this Eliot seems to have meant that the novelist's mind did not permit any prior formulation about experience to blind it to experience itself, that it did not attempt to arrive at any final generalization but remained alert to life's dialectical possibilities. In his essay "Shakespeare and the Stoicism of Senecia", Eliot is sceptical of "thinking", thought", "Ideas" or "philosophy" in art. As he says, the poet who thinks is merely the poet who can express the emotional equivalent of thought, but the poet is not necessarily interested in thought itself. In the same vein he writes later in the same essay :

> I would suggest that none of the plays of Shakespeare
> has a meaning, although it would be equally false to
> say that a play of Shakespeare is meaningless. All great
> poetry gives the illusion of a view of life.[14]

A great novel like any great piece of art does not present to us "Ideas"; it rather communicates a vision, a life and a world to us. "Ideas" in great art cannot exist in crude form; they can justify themselves in art only after being pulsated with sensation or feeling or the passionate capacity or what Eliot calls "sensuous apprehension" of the artist. Here we mark the clear-cut impact and imprint of F.H. Bradley. The "immediate experience" of F.H. Bradley points to the ideal state of equilibrium when thought and feeling or intellect and sensation interpenetrate or remain unified or closest to each other. Ideas in their raw form in art are like the dead lumber over it, blunting its sharper edge. They need to be in immediate contact with the senses, as we find in the "Immediate Experience". This is manifest from what Eliot writes on Henry James :

> In England ideas run wild and pasture on the emotions instead of thinking with feeling (a very different thing) we corrupt our feeling with ideas; we produce the political, the emotional idea, evading sensation and thought. George Meredith (the disciple of Carlyle) was fertile in "idea"; his epigrams are a facile substitute for observation and inference. Mr. Chesterton's brain swarms with ideas....James in his novels is like the best French critics in maintaining a viewpoint, a viewpoint untouched by the parasitic idea.[15]

James is a profound believer in the novel as a work of art and is, therefore, a confirmed opponent of any didacticism in fiction. James, nevertheless, infused into his work an important body of belief : the need for individual freedom and a moral vision, to be achieved through insight and awareness. "The conception of a certain young lady affronting her destiny" — that is how Henry James described the subject of *The Portrait of a Lady*.

Eliot regards novels, as he himself says, from the viewpoint of a poet. In other words, he examines them in the light of the perceptions gained in the composition of his own poetry. Eliot's earliest published reference to James occurs in a review he wrote while an undergraduate at Harvard. Speaking of Huneker's *Egoists* Eliot said that Huneker possessed a style which "shares with that of Mr. Henry James....what I should call a conversational quality; not conversational in admitting the slip-shod and madadroit or a meagre vocabulary, but by a certain informality, abandoning all the ordinary rhetorical hoaxes for securing attention."[16]

Eliot again connects James with the conversational style saying :

> The spoken and the written language must not be too near together as they must not be too far apart. Henry James's later style, for instance, is not exactly a conventional style....There is, however, an essential connection between the written and the spoken word, though it is not to be produced by aiming at a

conversational style in writing or a periodic style in speech : I have found this intimate, though indefinable connection between the speech and writing of every writer whom I have known personally who was a great writer....[17]

How highly Eliot regards Henry James is suggested by his having once placed that novelist's name along with those of Dante and Shakespeare. Eliot compares James with Dostoevsky :

I am inclined to think that the spirit of James, so much less violent, with so much more reasonableness and so much more resignation than that of the Russian, is no less profound, and is more useful, more applicable, for our future.[18]

Eliot extends his praise to Hawthorne and Henry James almost in an equal degree. He writes in "The Hawthorne Aspect"[19] that Hawthorne was deeply sensitive to the situation; that he grasped character through the relation of two or more persons to each other, and this is what no one less, except James, has done. He finds Hawthorne a finer stylist and a greater explorer of the soul than Mark Twain. He agrees with Henry James's opinion about Hawthorne : "The fine thing in Hawthorne is that he cared for the deeper psychology....".[20]

This definition, Eliot says, separates the two novelists (Henry James and Hawthorne) at once from their English contemporaries. Neither Dickens nor Thackeray had the smallest notion of the deeper psychology. George Eliot had a kind of heavy intellect for it.

Deeper psychology in the sense of inner, spiritual exploration, mental and emotional ramifications of the kind found in James and Hawthorne, is of course missing in most British novelists. It has no trace in Arnold Bennett, H.G. Wells, Galsworthy or Kipling. These novelists are, as Virginia Woolf terms them, "materialists".

Eliot says that Hawthorne and James have a kind of sense, a receptive medium, which is not of sight. It is not that they fail to make us see, so far as necessary, but sight is not the essential sense. They perceive by antennae; and a deeper psychology is present in them.

Eliot in his review called "American Literature"²¹ finds in Hawthorne both qualities — moral vision and the firmness, the true coldness, the hard coldness of the genuine artist. He seems to insist that in Hawthorne the degree of realism does not diminish owing to his observation of the moral life. The moral life in Hawthorne is to be understood in a wider sense, in terms of a deeper significance of human consciousness. He agrees with Professor Erskine's view that Hawthorne is no mystic and his method has no room for optimism and for prepossession of any kind. Eliot says that Hawthorne is really the questioner, the detached observer. He points out further that the observation of the moral life in *The Scarlet Letter, The House of the Seven Gables* and even in some of the tales and sketches has solidity, and permanence, the permanence of art. The work of Hawthorne is truly a criticism — true because of the fidelity of the artist and not merely because of the conviction of the man — of the Puritan morality, of the transcendental morality and of the world which Hawthorne knew. It is a criticism as Henry Janies's work is criticism of the America of his times, and as the work of Turgenev and Flaubert is a criticism of the Russia and the France of theirs. Thus, Eliot finds in Hawthorne capacity for enquiry, detached observation, and artistic integrity backed by a moral vision and the deeper psychology. Henry James and Hawthorne are almost the ideal novelists for Eliot.

In his essay "American Literature and the American Language" Eliot praises Mark Twain for discovering a new way of writing, valid not only for himself but for others. He places him, with Dryden and Swift, as one of those writers who brought their language up-to-date and thus, purified the dialect of the tribe. He appreciates *Huckkberry Finn* form the viewpoint of language only, though this novel deserves to be praised from other angles too. Mr. Henry Nash Smith in his introduction to *Adventures of Huckleberry Finn*²² says that *Huckleberry Finn* is, for all its imperfections, a great book, not only because it worked a revolution in American literary prose but because of what it is says against stupid conformity and slavery of the individual.

In his introduction to *Nightwood* by Djuna Barnes, Eliot says that it is a book of creative order which it is an impertinence to introduce. What is important in this novel is not one or two characters, one scene or one event, but the total, complete meaning, the pattern that emerges from the whole of the book. *Nightwood* is not just a collection of individual portraits, its characters are all knotted together by what we call Chance or Destiny. It is the whole pattern formed by the characters, rather than any individual constituent, that draws our interest. We come to know those characters through their effect on one another, and by what they say to one another about the others. Eliot adds :

> A prose that is altogether alive demands something of the reader that the ordinary novel-reader is not prepared to give. To say that *Nightwood* will appeal primarily to readers of poetry does not mean that it is not a novel; but that it is so good a novel that only sensibilities trained on poetry can wholly appreciate it. Miss Barnes's prose has prose rhythm that is prose style, and the musical pattern which is not that of verse. This prose rhythm may be more or less complex, or less complex or elaborate according to the purposes of the writers; but whether simple or complex, it is what raises the matter to be communicated to first intensity.[23]

Nightwood is a work of true creative imagination and not a philosophical treatise. Eliot finds, in the novel, a great achievement of style, beauty of phrasing, brilliance of wit and characterization, and a quality of horror and doom very nearly related to Elizabethan tragedy. He says that the book is not a psychopathic study. The miseries that people suffer through their particular abnormalities are visible on the surface, but the deeper design in the book is that of human misery and bondage which is universal.

Dr. F.R. Leavis writes critically of Eliot's enthusiastic review of Djuna Barnes's *Nightwood* :

> I have in mind writers in whom Eliot has expressed an interest in strongly favorable terms : Djuna Barnes of *Nightwood*, Henry Miller, Lawrence Durrell of *The Black Book*. In these writers — at any rate in the last two (and the first seems to' me insignificant) — the spirit of what we are offered affects me as being essentially a desire, in Laurentian phrase, to "do dirt" on life.[24]

In his review entitled "Beyle and Balzac" Eliot says that the great novelists make a patient analysis of human motives and emotions and dispense with atmosphere. This quality is to be found in Beyle, Flaubert and Dostoevsky rather than in Balzac. Apparently Beyle and Balzac both have imagination but the imagination in Balzac is much inferior to the former's. Imagination in Balzac coats and glosses over reality rather than brings light on it or peels off its appearances. The aura of Balzac has not a "clear, bright centre", it may rightly be called "mystical" but more truly "occult". In the greatest artist, says Eliot, imagination is a very different faculty from Balzac's : it becomes a fine, delicate tool for operation on the sensible world. Stendhal's scenes, and some of his phrases, read like cutting one's own throat; they are a terrible humiliation to read, in the understanding of human feelings and human illusions of feeling that they force upon the reader.

This exposure explains a great part of the superiority of Beyle and Flaubert over Balzac., Balzac, relying upon atmosphere, is capable of evading an issue, of satisfying himself with a movement or a word. Beyle and Flaubert, Eliot says, "strip the world" and they are men of far more than common intensity of feeling, of passion.

"Stendhal and Flaubert," says Eliot, "suggest unmistakably the awful separation between potential passion and any actualization possible in life. They indicate also the indestructible barriers between one human being and another."[25]

> It is this intensity, precisely, and consequent discontent with the inevitable inadequacy of actual living to the passionate capacity, which drove them to art and analysis. This surface of existence coagulates into lumps, which look like important simple feelings, which are identified by names as feelings which the patient analyst disintegrates into more complex or trifling, but ultimately, if he goes far enough, into various cancellations of something again simple, terrible and unknown.[26]

The aura of Balzac "sputters and goes out" when we compare Balzac's imagination with that of Dostoevsky. The imagination in Dostoevsky, as Eliot rightly points out, is utterly different, and put to utterly different uses. If we examine some of Dostoevsky's most — successful, most imaginative flights, we find them to be projection, continuations of the actual, the observed. In the final scene of *The Idiot*, and in the interview of Ivan Karmazov with the devil, Dostoevsky's point of departure is always a human brain in a human environment, and the aura is simply the continuation of the quotidian experience of the brain into seldom explored extremities of torture. But as most people are too unconscious of their own sufferings to suffer much, this continuation appears fantastic. Dostoevsky begins with the real world, as Beyle does; he pursues reality farther only in a certain direction. Balzac's imagination is not actually like a sharp-edged instrument to sink through the surface to the farthest and deepest reality of human life and the world. It is a phantasm that brings the forefront of reality more in shadow and darkness, cloak or cover. In Balzac, the fantastic element is of another sort. It is not an extension of reality, it is an atmosphere thrown upon reality direct from the personality of the writer. We cannot look at it, as we can look at anything in Dostoevsky. We ask ourselves in relation to what real, solid object the atmosphere of Balzac has meaning, the incantation is exposed to be powerless. The atmosphere of Balzac is the highest possible development of the atmosphere of Mrs. Radcliffe. In Dostoevsky Eliot finds "doubleness" and the "under-pattern" less manifest than the theatrical :

> We sometimes feel, in following the words and behaviours of some of the characters of Dostoevsky, that they are living at once on the plane that we know and on some, other plane of reality from which we are shut out; their behaviouor does not seem crazy, but rather in conformity with laws of some world that we cannot perceive.[27]

Eliot comments on Turgenev[28] while reviewing Edward Garnett's book on Turgenev. Turgenev, he says, is much more cosmopolitan than Goethe and is the least exploited of the Russian novelists. The novels of Turgenev compose a single work and one should study the whole of it. This insistence on the reading of the total work is typical of Eliot. He praises Edward

Garnett's book on Turgenev for the simple reason that it helps us to see his novels in relation to one another. Eliot says that the novels of Turgenev are one work in the sense that they are not a "series of scattered inspirations". Eliot says that Turgenev's is not a position of popular appeal. He finds him essentially the artist and not the showman. Turgenev to him is one who used Russian material naturally, with the simplicity of genius turning to what its feelings know best; he recognized in practice, at least, that a writer's art must be racial — which means, in plain words, that it must be based on the accumulated sensations of the first twenty-one years. Eliot praises Turgenev for his "insight into the universal sameness of men and women", his grasp on the uniformity of human nature, and more for the perfect proportion, the vigilant but not the theoretic intelligence and the "austere art of omission" :

> They (Turgenev's personages) are never unreal or abstract, but simply the essential. I am not sure that the method of Turgenev, this perfect proportion, this vigilant but never theoretic intelligence, this austere art of omission — is not that which in the end proves most satisfying to the civilized mind.[29]

Lord David Cecil also believes that it is the economical certainty of touch which gives Turgenev's pictures the continuous significance of art. Eliot notes in Turgenev's work not only this economy and proportion but also another important quality — an element of spirituality and a sense of the mystery of life. Eliot quotes approvingly Henry James's words on Turgenev :

> He carried about with him the air of feeling all the variety of life, of knowing strange and far-off things, of having a horizon in which the Parisian horizon easily lost itself....He was not all there, as the phrase is; he had something behind, in reserve.[30]

Eliot makes some general points about fiction. He says in his essay "Collins and Dickens" that a good novel should possess both dramatic as well as melodramatic elements, for melodrama is perennial and the craving for it is perennial, In modern times, terms like "high-brow fiction", "thrillers" and "detective fiction" are used to distinguish melodrama from drama, but in the Golden

Age of melodramatic fiction, says Eliot, there was no such distinction. The best novels were thrilling :

> We cannot afford to forget that the first and not one of the least difficult — requirements of either prose or verse is that it should be interesting.[31]

Eliot says the work of Wilkie Collins does not have the permanence of the greatest novels but one can learn something from it in "the art of interesting and exciting the reader." In the realm of novels, the possibilities of melodrama must, from time to time, be re-explored. The conventional method of thrilling has become stereotyped. The resources of Collins are, in comparison, inexhaustible. Great art is essentially the refinement of popular art :

> Collins's novels suggest questions which no student of the art of fiction can afford to neglect....Henry James....in his own practice could be not only interesting, but had a very cunning mastery of the finer melodrama....[32]

Mr. Walter Allen has written similarly, almost as if inspired by Eliot :

> The distinction between the entertainer and the novelist is a sophistication. There have been greater entertainers in fiction who have not been great novelists, but there has never been a great novelist who was not first of all a great entertainer, for the end of the novel, like that of poetry, is delight, and total significance, however, profoundly serious, will go for nothing, will not indeed exist, unless the novel has primary and overriding value as entertainment. That it should delight, whether at the most naive and unreflecting level or as a "superior amusement", is the first we ask of any novel.[33]

A comparative study of the novels of Wilkie Collins and Dickens can do much to illumininate the question of the difference between the dramatic and the melodramatic in fiction. Eliot seems to feel that Dickens is more melodramatic than Collins and Collins more dramatic than Dickens. Dickens in *Bleak House* tends towards Collins, as Collins *in The Woman in White* does towards Dickens.

Eliot praises Dickens for characterisation. He says that Dickens excelled in characters, in the creation of characters of greater intensity than even human beings. Collins was not usually strong in the creation of characters; but he was a master of plot and situation. The characters of Collins miss the typical quality of Dickensian characters. They are painstakingly coherent and life-like. Compared to Dicken's they lack the kind of reality which is almost suprenatural, which hardly seems to belong to the character by natural right, but seems rather to descend upon him by a kind of inspiration of grace. Eliot writes :

> Dickens's figures belong to poetry, like figures of Dante or Shakespeare, in that a single phrase, either by them or about them, may be enough to set them wholly before us.[34]

It is one of the important functions of a critic to revalue and rehabilitate the less known or the neglected writers in literature, and Eliot has partly performed this function by reviewing some novels of Wyndham Lewis.

That Eliot is favourably disposed to writing on Wyndham Lewis shows the similarity of temperament and the attitude of mind : Eliot is a classicist, an eschewer of sentimentality and he can hardly adjust himself with the biological mysticism of D.H. Lawrence. Wyndham Lewis belongs to the robust ethos of the nineteen-twenties and is, like Eliot, tough, masculine, virile. Despite the long neglect by the conventional critics, the genius of Wyndham Lewis was hailed by such masters as Eliot, Joyce and Pound.

Eliot reviewed *Tarr* in 1918, saying that it is a commonplace to compare Lewis to Dostoevsky. The method of Lewis, Eliot says, is, in fact, no more like that of Dostoevsky, taking *Tarr* as a whole, than it is like that of Flaubert. To compare Lewis to Dostoevsky, says Eliot, is not very useful because Lewis's mind is different and his aims are different.

In contrast to Dostoevsky, Lewis is impressively deliberate, even frigid. There is a peculiar intellectuality not akin to that of Flaubert. Intelligence, however, as Eliot says, is only a part of Lewis's quality; it is united with a vigorous physical organism which interests itself directly in sensation for its own sake. The direct contact with the senses, the perfection of the world of immediate experience with its own scale of values, is like Dostoevsky, but there is always the suggestion of a purely intellectual curiosity in the senses. And there is another important quality — humour.

There can be no question of the importance of *Tarr*. But it is only in part a novel : for the rest, Mr. Lewis is a magician who compels our interest in himself : he is the most fascinating personality of our time rather than a novelist. The artist, I believe, is more primitive, as well as more civilized, than his contemporaries, his experience is deeper than civilization, and he only uses the phenomena of civilization in expressing it. Primitive instincts and the acquired babits of ages are confounded in the ordinary man. In the work of Mr. Lewis, we recognize the thought of the modern and the energy of the caveman.[35]

Eliot wrote a note on *Monstre Ga*i by Wyndham Lewis in *The Hudson Review*[36] in 1955. In his review of *Tarr,* he finds some similarity between Wyndham Lewis and Dostoevsky and, in his note on *Monstre Gai*, he says that Wyndham Lewis has something common with Henry James in the novelty of style. He regards him as a "distinguished living English novelist" and as the "greatest prosemaster of style" who can set "one's sluggish brain in motion".

Eliot points out that *Monstre Gai* is a sequel or continuation of *The Childermass*, and Monstre Gai also is to have a sequel. He adds that *Monstre Gai* is much better than its forerunner *The Childermass*, not only in construction but also in the story elements, the characterisation, in the measure of reality and its maturity. *The Childermss* compared to *Monstre Gai* strikes most readers as a brilliant, interminably long opening chapter. The reader's attention is held by the power of the style, the vividness of the pictures, and the brilliance of the debate. *Monstre Gai* on the other hand, tells a story, and is filled with what it is an understatement to call exciting episodes.

Beyond the structural improvement, the much greater skill at plain story-telling, Eliot finds here a more important difference.

There is, it seems to Eliot, a gain in maturity in *Monstre Gai.*
The difference in maturity, says Eliot, between *The Childermass*
and *Monstre Gai* is not merely that the philosophy in the latter
is riper or more explicit or more coherent; there is, he believes,
also a development in humanity. In the first part of *The*
Childermass one is too often reminded that Pulley and Satters
belong to Mr. Lewis's puppet gallery. It is not that their creator
failed to make them real — it is that he denied them more than
a measure of reality. In *Monstre Gai,* the puppets, says Eliot,
begin to get the better of the puppet-master, and become human
beings.

Lewis was a painter, a draughtsman, and a writer, but such
a range of powers is easily dismissed as virtuosity — implying
that a man who does several things must do all of them badly.
Eliot says one cannot treat Lewis like that, any more than one
can Goethe or Leonardo. In his pictures and in his prose, Lewis
sought all his life to explore the possibilities of a number of
different forms of expression.

> As for the novel it is wellknown that I am not a novel.
> reader, that there are notable novelists with whose work
> I have only a partial acquaintance, and others with
> whose work I have no expectation of acquainting myself
> at all : so that I can only, suspect" that Mr. Lewis is
> the most distinguished living English novelist....There
> are some writers who please me because they seem to
> hold the same views as myself, others who annoy me
> by maintaining opinions that seem to me manifestly
> silly; but very few who can set my sluggish brain in
> motion, and for that I am always grateful. The opinion
> to which I do not hesitate to commit myself is that
> Mr. Lewis is the greatest prose-master of style of my
> generation — perhaps the only one to have invented a
> new style. And by style I do not mean "craftsmanship"
> nor do I impute "impeccability"....I have observed that
> Mr. Lewis has this in common with Henry James....[37]

F.R. Leavis is critical of Eliot's appraisal of Wyndham Lewis.
He writes :

> Yet I cannot believe that he (Eliot) could have
> committed himself to such extravagant appraisals of this

last (Lewis) as a creative writer and a thinker if he had not known him personally (one tries to give Eliot credit for a kind of loyalty that is not at all a virtue in a critic as such)...."[38]

Eliot is almost lyrical in his praise of *Ulysses*. He says that Joyce's parallel use of the *Odyssey* in this book has a great importance. The method has the importance of a "scientific discovery". No one else built a novel on such a foundation before : it had never been necessary. Eliot finds in *Ulysses* a new method for the adequate rendering of the "immense panorama which is contemporary history" with precision and compression. Eliot takes *Ulysses* as a novel and more than a novel. To call *Ulysses* an epic is not to diminish its importance. *Ulysses* is not a novel, says Eliot, simply because the novel is a form which will no longer serve, and because the novel, instead of being a form, was simply the expression of an age.

Mr. Joyce his written one novel — *The Portrait*; and Mr. Wyndham Lewis has written one novel — *Tarr*. I do not suppose that either of them will ever write another novel. The novel ended with Flaubert and with James. It is, I think, because Mr. Joyce and Mr. Lewis, being in advance of their time, felt a conscious or probably unconscious dissatisfaction with the form, that their novels are more formless than those of a dozen clever writers who are unaware of its obsolescence.[39]

In using the myth, in manipulating a continuous parallel between "contemporaneity and antiquity", Eliot says James Joyce is simply devising a way of controlling, of ordering. of giving a shape and a significance to the "immense panorama of futility and anarchy which is contemporary history". Joyce is pursing a method which others must pursue after him. They will not be imitators any more than the scientist who uses the discoveries of an Einstein in pursuing his own, independent, further investigation. The method in *Ulysses* is one for which the horoscope is auspicious. Instead of the narrative method, says Eliot, one may now use the mythical method. It is, as he seriously believes, a step towards making the modern world possible for art.

Eliot does not examine *Ulysses* as a whole. He concentrates on its method and commends it as a discovery and formula for compressing the multifarious and multitudinous experiences that confront and envelop the modern man. Dr. F.R. Leavis does not see *Ulysses* in as favourable a light as Eliot :

> But it seems plain to me that there is no organic principle determining, informing and controlling into a vital whole, the elaborate and analogical structure, the extraordinary variety of technical devices, the attempts at an exhaustive rendering of consciousness for which *Ulysses* is remarkable, and which got it accepted by a cosmopolitan literary world as a new start. It is rather, I think, a dead end or at least a pointer to disintegration — a view strengthened by Joyce's own development....[40]

Eliot writes in his essay on Swinburne that the prose of James Joyce or the earlier Conrad is important as it is struggling to digest and express new objects, new feelings, new aspects. In a Commentary in the *Criterion*,[41] he says that Joseph Conrad is unquestionably a great novelist, endowed with the modesty as well as the conviction of a great writer. Conrad's reputation is as secure as that of any writer of his time: critical analysis, says Eliot, may adjust but it will not diminish his importance.

Eliot wrote an obituary[42] on Virginia Woolf, in which he spoke highly of her. Virginia Woolf's imaginative genius and her sense of style, Eliot says, cannot be contested. Eliot dwells upon the qualities of personal charm and distinction, of kindliness and wit, of curiosity about human beings as well as the particular advantage of a kind of hereditary position (with the incidental benefits which the position bestowed) of Virginia Woolf. But one will be led to a false impression if one makes much of th "accidental advantage" of Virginia Woolf, for "her fame itself is solidly enough built upon the writings".

He points out that Virginia Woolf was the centre not merely of an esoteric group, but of the literary life of London. "Her position was due to a concurrence of qualities and circumstances which never happened before....It maintained the dignified and admirable tradition of Victorian upper middleclass culture — a situation in which the artist was neither the servant of the exalted patron, nor the parasite of the plutocrat, nor the entertainer of the mob — a situation in which the producer and the consumer of art were on equal footing, and neither the highest nor the lowest. With the death of Virginia Woolf, a whole pattern of culture is broken. She may be, from one point of view, only the symbol, of it; but she would not be the symbol, if she had not been, more than any one in her time, the maintainer of it."[43]

F. R. Leavis is critical of Eliot for praising James Joyce and Virginia Woolf and under-valuing D.H. Lawrence he writes "His (Eliot's) performance as a judge of his contemporaries has been consistently disastrous. It is represented at its most respectable by his backing Joyce — the significance of which election, all the same, is given in his dismissal of Lawrence."[44] And later :

> What I myself was slow, I confess, to realise was that Eliot was as completely of that Bloomsbury world in acceptance and loyalty or docility....The absurd (and orthodox) over-estimate of Virginia Woolf implied in his references to her might seem to be a natural and spontaneous aberration, closely correlated with his unquestionably and profoundly personal prepossessions against D.H. Lawrence ("*non — seulement est elle civilisée elle préfere la civilization à la barbarie*", "not only is she civilized, she prefers civilisation to barbarism", he wrote in a "letter" to *La Nouvelle Révue Francaise*), yet contemplating the strikingly unguarded and uncharacteristic rashness with which he indulges prepossession in emphatic, righteous, and indefensible pronouncements of overtly damning intention at Lawrence's expense, we have to remind ourselves that in this prepossession too there was Bloomsbury with him....[45]

Eliot in *After Strange Gods* is critical of Hardy's and Lawrence's novels. It is quite expected of Eliot that he should not be favourably disposed to the emotional intensity of Hardy's work. It appears that Eliot has not done due justice to Hardy. Eliot finds in Hardy only extreme emotionalism, writing only for "self-expression", "exploitation of personality", self-absorption, and symptoms of decadence. Eliot further points out that the work of Thomas Hardy represents an interesting example of a powerful personality uncurbed by any institutional attachment or by submission to any objective beliefs, Hardy essentially and finally stands for forthright sincerity, integrity, devotion, utmost sacrifice, and genuine love. His work points to idealism, paganism and liberalism, and to these, the classicist, the formalist and the orthodox in T.S. Eliot cannot give approving response. Hardy's vision, Hardy's belief — that happiness is but an occasional episode in the general drama of pain, or "As flies to wanton boys, are we to the Gods; they kill us for their sport" — cannot be called mere fancy or phantasm and is not without the objectivity of proper observation. A man in moments of solitude may feel drawn to pondering over the mystery of the universe and the littleness and nothingness of man against the force of Fate or the tremendous powers of God. It seems unfair on the part of Eliot to say that Hardy represents "emotional paroxysms" or "passion for its own sake".

> He seems to me to have written as nearly for the sake of self-expression, as a man well can; and the self which he had to express does not strike me as a particularly wholesome or edifying matter of communication....At times his style touches sublimity....Landscape, too, is filled for the purposes of an author who is interested not at all in men's minds, but only in their emotion and perhaps only in men as vehicles for emotion. This extreme emotionalism seems to me a symptom of decadence; it is a cardinal point of faith in a Romantic age, to believe that there is something admirable in violent emotion for its own sake, whatever the emotion or whatever. Its emotion or whatever its object....People imagine passion to be the surest evidence of vitality. This in itself may go towards according for Hardy's popularity.[46]

But Eliot is right in pointing out a flaw in the work of Hardy. What introduces a note of falsity into Hardy's novels is that he leaves nothing to nature, but always gives one last turn of the screw himself, and Eliot has the gravest suspicion, of his motives for so doing. In *The Mayor of Casterbridge* — which has always seemed to Eliot his finest novel as a whole — he comes nearest to producing an air of inevitability, and of making crises seem the consequences of the character of Henchard; the arrangement by which the hero, leaning over a bridge, finds himself staring at his effigy in the stream below is masterly *tour de force*. This scene is however as much by arrangement as less successful ones in which the motives intrude themselves more visibly; as for instance, the scene in *Far from the Madding Crowd* in which Bathsheba unscrews Fanny Robin's coffin — which seems to him deliberately fake.

The strictures of Eliot regarding D.H. Lawrence are well-known. Eliot confesses his prejudice regarding Lawrence but he cannot help it. His attitude to Lawrence in *After Strange Gods* and elsewhere in his reviews or introductions is almost the same, Eliot in *After Strange Gods* regards D.H. Lawrence "a very much greater genius, if not a greater artist than Hardy", yet he finds in him the lack of a sense of humour, a lack not so much of information as of the critical facilities which education should give and an incapacity for what we ordinarily call, "thinking". Of this side of Lawrence, Eliot says, there is the brilliant exposure by Wyndham Lewis in *Paleface*. Eliot finds in the work of D.H. Lawrence a "distinct sexual morbidity" and an, insensibility to ordinary social morality" — and he calls this a 'monstrosity", He argues that Lawrence started life wholly free from any restriction of tradition, that he had no guidance except the untrustworthy and deceitful guide called the Inner Light. The deplorable religious upbringing gave Lawrence a lust for intellectual independence. Lawrence had keen sensibility and capacity for profound intuition, but from this intuition, says Eliot, he drew the wrong conclusions. Lawrence with his acute sensibility, violent prejudices and passions and lack of intellectual and social training is admirably fitted to be an instrument for the forces of good or evil. Eliot calls D.H. Lawrence "an untrained mind" and a soul "destitute of humanity" and filled with self-righteousness, "a blind servant" and "a fatal leader". He says that Lawrence was right in speaking again and again against the living death of modern material civilization. And as a criticism of the modern world *Fantasia of the Unconscious* is a book to keep at hand for re-reading.

Eliot does not find any development in *Lady Chatterley's Lover*; the game-keeper is representative of "social obsession", which makes well-born or almost well-born ladies offer themselves to plebeians, and this springs, says Eliot, from the same morbidity which makes other female characters of Lawrence bestow their favours upon savages. He finds the author of *Lady Chatterley's Lover* "a very sick man indeed".

There is, Eliot believes, a very great deal to be learnt from Lawrence but he fears that Lawrence's work may appeal, not to those who are well and able to discriminate, but to the sick and debile and confused; and not to what remains of health in them but to their sickness. Concerning Lawrence, Eliot has even used words like "rotten and rotting others". Though at one time Eliot called Lawrence "a serious and an improving writer", it is a fact that he never adjusted with him. Lawrence has never drawn a fully favourable response from Eliot.

One may remark that it is not fair on the part of Eliot to slight a novelist of such tremendous creative gifts. Lawrence has indeed a great range of powers; he has delicacy, subtlety, intuition, forthright language, superb imagination and much human tenderness. Lawrence says in his essay "Morality and Novel" : "The novel can help us to live, as nothing else can."

In praise of Lawrence, Aidous Huxley has written a brilliant introduction to the letters of Lawrence selected by Richard Aldington. He says that Lawrence was in a real sense possessed by his creative genius. He emphasises the significant statement of Lawrence himself that "one has to be terribly religious to be an artist". He is right in pointing out that Lawrence's special and characteristic gift was an extraordinary sensitiveness to what Wordsworth called "unknown modes of being". Lawrence could never forget, as most of us almost continuously forget, the dark presence of the otherness that lies beyond the boundaries of man's conscious mind. And this special sensibility was accompanied by an immense power of rendering and registering the immediately experienced otherness in terms of literary art.

E.M. Forster in *Aspects of the Novel* is lyrical in his praise of Lawrence, He finds Lawrence the only living novelist in whom "the song predominates", who has the "rapt bardic quality", and whom "it is idle to criticize".

F.R. Leavis has brilliantly criticised Eliot's arguments and statements on Lawrence in his essays "The Wild Untutored

Phoenix" and "Eliot, Wyndham Lewis and Lawrence", included in *The Common Pursuit*. He points out the pertinent fact that Lawrence knew four languages besides his own and had an extremely wide and close acquaintance with painting, too. Lawrence did not exactly suffer from lack of social, intellectual and educational training; at twenty-one he was no less an intellectual than Eliot at the same age. Dr. Leavis finds in him not only what we "ordinarily call thinking" but an extraordinarily penetrating, persistent and vital kind of thinking.

> I have already intimated that the acuteness of Lawrence's sensibility seems to me (whatever Bloomsbury may have decided) inseparable from the play of a supremely fine and penetrating intelligence.... but few readers of the memoir of Lawrence, by E.T. will, I imagine, however expensive their own education, claim with any confidence that they had a better one than Lawrence had.[47]

And later :

> Eliot's stress in this book (*After Strange Gods*) falls explicitly upon the religious needs of the age....When, for instance, he says that he is applying 'moral principles to literature', we cannot accept those principles as alternative to the criteria we know....

> This equivocalness, this curious sleight by which Eliot surreptitiously takes away while giving, is what I mean by the revealingly uncritical in his attitude towards Lawrence.

> And for attributing to him "spiritual sickness" Mr. Eliot can make out a strong case. But it is characteristic of the world as it is, that health cannot anywhere be found whole; and the sense in which Lawrence stands for health is an important one. He stands at any rate for something, without which the preoccupation (necessary as it is) with order, forms, and deliberate construction, cannot produce health.[48]

However, one feels that Matthew Arnold would hardly have included D.H. Lawrence in his list of classics. Lawrence has perhaps genuineness but not greatness, and Eliot is right in saying that the greatness of literature is to be judged not by literary standards alone. Eliot is not wholly wrong about Lawrence when he finds in him "the tragic waste of powers". In spite of the utmost lyrical sensibility, the imaginative apprehension and gift of language, one has a feeling of vacuity and one desires that Lawrence's genius should have worked upon some different, intenser stuff and experience of life.

The attitude to the novel held by Eliot in the essay "Religion and Literature" may be questioned and criticized. The ethics and the morals that Eliot here talks of are narrow, purely Christian; and not always unacceptable. Eliot writes : "I am not concerned here with religious literature but with the application of our religion to the criticism of any literature."

Eliot says that it is quite irrational to separate literary judgments from our religious ones, but one can add that it is equally irrational to impose a purely Christian judgment on literature. Eliot feels sad to note the "gradual secularization" of the novel. Bunyan and to some extent Defoe, says Eliot, bad moral purposes. But since Defoe, Eliot adds, the "secularization" of the novel has been continuous.

> There have been three chief phases. In the first, the novel took the Faith, in its contemporary version, for granted and omitted it from its picture of life. Fielding, Dickens and Thackeray belong to this phase. In the second, it doubted, worried about, or contested the Faith. To this phase belong George Eliot, George Meredith and Thomas Hardy. To the third phase, in which we are living, belong nearly all contemporary novelists except Mr. James Joyce. It is the phase of those who have never heard the Christian Faith spoken of as anything but an anachronism.[49]

The critical approach here is not that of scientific, dispassionate enquiry. If Eliot takes the "secularization' of the novel as an unhappy feature, the baptization of fiction is still more disastrous and unwelcome in literature. Any good literature should of course be 'moral" but in the sense suggested by Henry James. In his preface to *The Portrait of a Lady*, Henry James remarks that the moral sense of a work of art depends on the amount of felt life concerned in producing it. He says that the "developing air of the artist's humanity" gives the last touch to a work of art.

F. R. Leavis also deals with the association of literature and morality and examines certain novelists in this light. But the moral intensity of Dr. Leavis is unlike Eliot's attitude in "Religion and Literature". It is the result of, and distinguished by, a vital capacity for experience and a kind of reverent openness before life.

Regarding Eliot's criticism of the novel and novelists, it is worth noting that :

(i) Eliot's criticism of the novel is not criticism proper, It is review, interpretation or, in Eliot's own phrase, "literary journalism"; yet it is significant.

(ii) It has not been written systematically according to a plan or a major point of view, as F.R. Leavis has done in *The Great Tradition.*

(iii) It is often of a far too general kind. Eliot does not examine the novels in detail.

(iv) Eliot's opinions on novelists are, in one sense, incidental; Eliot wrote about novels only when he had to write reviews.

(v) As he himself says, Eliot examines novels from the viewpoint of a verse-maker. In other words, he searches the novels for a method, for a language, for some clue or suggestion that may be helpful to a poet in the composition of poetry. For example, Eliot appreciates the method of compression and controlling in *Ulysses* which could be a stimulus to the making of a poem like *The Waste Land.* He also says that the language of Joyce and Conrad is important as it is struggling to digest new groups of feeling or new groups of objects or experiences.

(vi) Eliot likes novels that have a pattern formed not by one or two characters but by the whole book. The total meaning emerging from the novel is more important to him than any of its constituents.

REFERENCES

1. F.R. Leavis, "Eliot's Stature as Critic", *Commentary XXVI,* November 1958, p. 405.
2. Eliot's Introduction, *The Wheel of Fire,* 1954, p. xiii.

3. *Ibid.*
4. "Eliot on Henry James", *PMLA*, September 1984, p. 490.
5. *Aspects of the Novel, Penguin,* 1968, p. 154.
6. *Ibid.,* p. 162.
7. "In Memory of Henry James", *Egoist,* V. I (January 1918), 1-2.
8. *Explorations,* 1958, p. I (Chatto & Windus).
9. *The Calendar of Modern Letters,* October 1926.
10. *The English Novel,* Pelican Book, p. 16.
11. Eliot : "In Memory of Henry James" (1918), reprinted in *The Little Review,* V, 4 (August 1918), 44-47; "A Prediction" (1924) by Eliot, (included in) *A Collection of Critical Essays,* ed. by Leon Edel.
12. "A Prediction in Regard to Three English Authors, who though Masters of Thought, are likewise Masters of Art," *Vanity Fair,* XXI, 6 (February 1924), 29, 98.
13. *Ibid.*
14. *Selected Essays,* p. 135.
15. "In Memory", *The Shock of Recognition,* ed. by Edmund Wilson.
16. Eliot's untitled review in *The Harvard Advocate,* LXXXVIII (5 October 1909), 16.
17. "Charles Whibley", *Selected Essays.*
18. "A Prediction", by Eliot, *Vanity Fair,* XXI. 6 (February 1924), 98.
19. "The Hawthorne Aspect", *The Little Review,* V. 4 (August 1918), 47-53.
20. *Ibid.*
21. *Athenaeum,* 26 April, 1919, 236-37.
22. *The Adventures of Huckleberry Finn,* Riverside Edition, 1958.
23. *The Criterion,* Vol. XVI, No. 64, April 1937, p. 560.
24. *The Great Tradition, Penguin,* 1967, p. 36.
25. Quoted by Hugh Kenner, *The Invisible Poet : T. S. Eliot,* London, 1960, p. 78.
26. *Ibid.*
27. *Selected Essays,* p. 229.
28. *Egoist,* IV. 11 (December 1917), p. 167.
29. *Ibid.*
30. *Ibid.*
31. *Selected Essays,* p. 470.
32. *Ibid.*
33. W. Allen, *The English Novel* (Pelican), 1954, p. 159.
34. *Selected Essays,* p. 462.
35. *Egoist,* Vol., 8 (September 1918), 105-6.
36. *The Hudson Review,* Winter 1955, Vol. VII, No. 4, p. 400.

37. *Ibid.*

38. "Eliot's Stature as Critic", *Commentary*, XXVI, November 1958, p. 404.

39. *Ulysses*, reviewed by Eliot, *Dial*, LXXV, 5 (November 1923), p. 480.

40. *The Great Tradition*, Penguin, 1967, p. 36.

41. *The Criterion*, Vol. 111, No. 9, Oct. 1924.

42. *Horizon*, 17 (May, 1941), pp. 313-16.

43. *Ibid.*, p. 316.

44. *Commentary*, XXVI, November 1958, p. 405.

45. *Ibid.*

46. *Selected Prose*, ed. by John Hayward, Penguin, pp. 196-97.

47. "The Wild Untutored Phoenix", *The Common Pursuit*, Penguin, 1952, p. 235.

48. "Eliot, Wyndham Lewis and Lawrence", *The Common Pursuit*, pp. 240-42, 245-47.

49. *Selected Fssays*, p. 392.

7

Style of the Master

"Literary criticism," wrote Lawrence, "can be no more than a reasoned account of the feelings produced upon the critic by the book he is criticising. Criticism can never be a science : it is, in the first place, much too personal, and in the second, it is concerned with values that science ignores. The touchstone is emotion, not reason. We judge a work of art by its effect on our sincere and vital emotion, and nothing else...."[1]

The detection, therefore, of the nature of one's style, in criticism as well as in creative work, demands from us a thorough, constant and comprehensive grasp and study, because style is not an external trick or mannerism or superficial decoration imposed from without. Style is like the essence or the fragrance which wholly pervades the flower. It springs from the kind of content, idea, nature of experience, the outlook or the vision, the nature and the temperament that the writer possesses. The hackneyed statement — "The style is the man" — has every grain of truth.

Stories are told of scrupulous writers, like Flaubert, who spent days trying to get one or two sentences exactly right. Command over words is ultimately command over life and experience. Maupassant reports Flaubert as saying : "Whatever, the thing is that one wishes to say, there is only one word to express it, one verb to animatce it, and one adjective to qualify it. Therefore, one must search until one has found them, this word, this verb, this adjective."

Before we raise the essential points regarding the chief features of study manifested in Eliot's critical and non-critical prose, it will not be superfluous to dwell a little more upon style itself.

Middleton Murry points out in his book, *The Problem of Style*, that style means that "personal idiosyncrasy of expression" by which we recognise a writer.

> It is certain that no amount of correctness in grammar and composition is enough to make a positive style, even in the sense of technique of expression....Here then we have three fairly distinct meanings of the word "style" disengaged; style as personal idiosyncrasy; style as technique of exposition; style as the highest achievement of literature.[2]

Middleton Murry's phrase "personal idiosyncrasy" denotes what constitutes the characteristic, individual way of expression, mode, behaviour or gesture in the communication of ideas. We find, in Eliot's entire prose work, this "personal idiosyncrasy" or the individual mode of writing which is Eliot's and none other's. We can recognise and ascribe an anonymous piece of writing to Eliot, if we have studied, and apprehended his other writings; as we know an intimate from a distance by his peculiar gait, the rhythm of his movement, even when his face is not fully visible to us.

There is a marked difference between the essays of Eliot which were actually delivered as lectures and the essays not meant to be so. The difference between the two kinds of essays is the difference natural to writing and to speech. But the fact is that the quality of speech or rhetoric, the immediate sense of the audience, the informal tone of the address, the art of convincing, cajoling and persuading the reader is everywhere in Eliot's essays. And one more difference is to be noted between the early essays and the later ones. In the early essays of Eliot, one finds a greater degree of orthodoxy, convinction, vigour, and incisive analysis, and an attempt to see the obiect as it is. Hence, the early essays have a greater degree of surety than the later ones and are more exciting and persuasive. Eliot says in his essays "To Criticise the Critic" :

> There are errors of judgment, and what I regret more there are errors of tone : the occasional note of arrogance, of vehemence, cocksureness or rudeness, the braggadacio of the mild-mannered man safely entrenched behind his typewriter....[3]

So far I can judge....it is my earlier essays which have made the deeper impression. I attribute this to two causes. The first is the dogmatism of youth. When we are young we see issues sharply defined, as we age we tend to make more reservations, to qualify our positive assertions, to introduce more parentheses....We regard the enemy with greater tolerance. And when we are young, we are confident in our opinions....The second reason for the enduring popularity of some of my early criticism is....that....I was implicitly defending the sort of poetry that I and my friends wrote. This gave my essays a kind of urgency, the warmth of the appeal of the advocate which my later, more detached and I hope judicial essays, cannot claim."[4]

The style of Eliot is at its best in the essays on the Metaphysicals, "Dante", "Tradition and the Individual Talent", "Poetry and Drama", and on F.H. Bradley and the Elizabethan dramatists. Eliot is not a "creative" critic like Lord David Cecil, nor a "Romantic" critic like Walter Pater or Arthur Symons. The critical method and style in Eliot's criticism are generally analytical, incisive, anatomical, scientific and expository.

One of the important features of Eliot's style in prose is its liveliness. Eliot's style brings to us a sense of familiarity, of amiability, and thus, commands our greater co-operation and goodwill; this quality points, at the same time, to the inner poise and strength of conviction of the writer. Humour in Eliot's style is a functional weapon that Eliot wields, attacking the fallacious and establishing the truth. Miss M.C. Bradbrook says in her essay that Eliot's style "works much in terms of negative, and of definition by exclusion". At the end of his essay, "Wilkie Collins and Dickens" Eliot states that one of the first requirements of either prose or verse is that it should be "interesting". In his essay on Dryden, he says that "the prospect of delight alone justifies the perusal "of poetry". He informs[5] us about Charles Whibley that he had the first requisite of a critic : an interest in his subject, and ability to arouse an interest for it. Eliot performs almost the same task : he makes his prose delightful and interesting through different means — through the conversational tone, humour and wit, and by communicating the note of surprise and the sense of contrast. A piece of lively and interesting prose may be taken as an example :

> There is, however, one contemporary figure about whom my mind will, I fear, always waver between dislike, exasperation, boredom and admiration — that is D.H. Lawrence.
>
> My opinions of D.H. Lawrence seem to form a tissue of praise and execration. The vehemence of my ejaculations of dislike are perserved, like flies in amber, or like wasps in honey, by the diligence of Dr. Leavis....Last year, in the Lady Chatterley case, I expressed my readiness to appear as a witness for the defence. Perhaps the counsel for the defence were well-advised not to Put me into the witness-box, as it might have been rather difficult to make my views clear to a jury by that form of inquisition, and a really wily prosecutor might tie me up in knots. I felt then, as I feel now, that the prosecution of such a book, a book of most serious and highly moral intention, was a deplorable blunder, the consequencess of which would be most unfortunate, whatever the verdict, and give the book a kind of vogue which would have been abhorrent to the author. But my antipathy to the author remains, on the ground of what seems to me egotism, a strain of cruelty and a feeling in common with Thomas Hardy — a lack of a sense of humour.[6]

Close examination of this passage shows many qualities which are typical of Eliot's style. The passage exhibits the firmness and conviction of a viewpoint. Here the tone of conviction is one of the chief sources of the strength of style. The lines delight us but also seem to destroy the opponent's point of view. They ridicule and belittle. "Like flies in amber, or like wasps in honey, by the diligence of Dr. Leavis' reminds us of the process in Pope's ironical verses. And Leavis's seriously written book in defence of D.H. Lawrence seems to lose, for a moment, its force, edge and seriousness in our imagination. Though Eliot is usually a man of humility, he is not always without haughtiness : M.C. Bradbook in her essay has rightly noted the "haughty humility" in Eliot. In this passage Eliot seems to speak from an Olympian height and presents the criticism of Dr. Leavis about Lawrence in a somewhat demeaning light. The word "diligence" brings associations of physical labour. By the ironic and witty use of a single sentence, or a word, Eliot is able to petrify or impoverish his adversary. Dr. Leavis does not usually have this fund of humour, the jocular ironic turns and twists of phrases which are a continual delight in reading Eliot's prose. Dr. Leavis is nothing if not very serious and sombre.

Eliot says that a poet has a three-fold problem to solve : he must earn a living, he must practise and perfect himself in writing, and he must cultivate other interests as well.

> I do not think any parents have ever brought a child up with a view to his becoming a poet; some parents have brought up their children to be criminals; but for good and loving parents a poet is almost the last thing they could want their child to be, unless they thought it was the only way of saving him becoming a criminal.[7]

One marks the typical jocular, ironic and ridiculing tone and style in Eliot's review[8] of Bertrand Russell's *Why I am not a Christian in The Criterion*. Eliot first of all quotes Russell's words :

> We want to stand upon our own feet and look fair and square at the world — its good facts, its bad facts, its beauties and ugliness, see the world as it is, and be not afraid of it, conquer the world by intelligence and not merely by being slavishly subdued by the terror that comes from it.[9]

Eliot makes fun of Russell for his keenness in looking at things "fair and square" and "on standing rather sitting down". He argues that Russell has wholly unreasoning prejudice in favour of freedom, kindliness and such things. He agrees with him that fear is a bad thing but at the same time he protests that fear has several shades of meaning and the fear of God is quite different from the fear of burglary or bankruptcy. He says that there is good and bad fear of God; the bad way of fearing God is the way that stimulates toxins in the blood, producing horripilation.

Eliot's style cannot be called, to use Alan Warner's words, "the gritty style".[10] Benjamin Franklin once answered his own question, "What qualities should a writing have to be good and perfect of its kind", by saying that it should be "smooth, clear and short". Eliot's style in his best critical essays is one of analysis and elucidation. Remarking, "....He (Swinburne) uses the most general word, because his emotion is never particular, never in direct line of vision, never focused...."[11] Eliot quotes the line of Swinburne :

> There lived a singer in France of old
> By the tideless dolorous midland sea.
> In a land of sand and ruin and gold
> There shone one woman, and none but she.

Eliot continues :

....Swinburne defines the place in the most general word, which has for him its own value. "Gold", "ruin", "dolorous"; it is not merely the sound that he wants. but the vague associations of ideas that the words give him. He has not his eye on a particular place....[12]

In a brilliant critical analysis in "From Poe to Valéry", he writes :

> Poe had, to an exceptional degree, the feeling for the incantatory element in poetry. but in his choice of. the right sound Poe is by no means careful that it should have also the right sense. I will give one comparison of uses of the same by Poe and by Tennyson....
>
> [Poc's lines] :
> It was night, in the lonesome October
> Of my most immemorial year....
>
> "Immemorial" according to the Oxford Dictionary, means : "that is beyond memory, or out of mind; ancient beyond memory or a record : extremely old". None of these meanings seems applicable to this use of word by Poe. The year was not beyond the memory, the speaker remembers one incident very well.
>
> [The line of Tennyson] :
> The moan of doves in immemorial elms.

Here "immemorial", besides having the most felicitous sound value, is exactly the word for trees so old that no one knows just how old they are.[13]

Eliot's style is also somewhat rhetorical in the best sense of the term. "The word [rhetoric] simply cannot be used as synonymous with bad writing....Let us avoid the assumption that rhetoric is vice of manner, and endeavour to find a rhetoric of substance also, which is right because it issues from what it has to express."[14]

And the element of rhetoric in the prose style of Eliot has no suggestion of verbiage; it calls for insistence and emphasis on the central point — the point which Eliot likes to communicate to the reader with strength, directness and force. The rhetorical manner in Eliot conveys in the end an effect "not of verbosity, but of bold, even shocking....directness".

The language of Eliot's earlier critical essays, though compact is rhetorical, almost in the debater's style. The compact, method of rhetoric, expansion and elaboration in the earlier essays helps Eliot a great deal in rejecting and negating the conventional, pseudo-Romantic Georgian modes and in establishing new emphases in criticism. The rhetoric in "Tradition and the Individual Talent" is not the vice of manner; it is a rhetoric of substance in the sense that it issues from what the writer has to express. The repetition of "the historical sense" in "Tradition and the Individual Talent" brings to the reader the sense of functional rhetoric. Some words sometimes need to be repeated :

> It involves, in the first place, the historical sense, which we may call indispensable....and the historical sense involves a perception not only of the pastness of the past....the historical sense compels a man to write not merely....this historical sense which is a sense of the timeless as well as of the temporal....[15]

In the same manner there is the recurrence of the word "mind" for four or five times in a single line of the same essay :

He must be aware that the mind of Europe — the mind of his own country — a mind which he learns in time to be much more important than his own private mind — is a mind which changes.[16]

Henri Fluchére in an essay says that Valéry, compared to Eliot, is too much of a conscious artist, he is far more preoccupied with the way in which he puts a statement than with the statement itself. Eliot's prose, M. Fluchére continues, is never more than the best possible way of communicating his thought (exactly what Middleton Murry describes as style) — and does not want to be more.

Eliot's style proceeds slowly, is often repetitive, and not seldom far from easy-going, as an instrument of investigation should be, which should not leave any stone unturned, any hypothesis untried, and yet reach the conclusion with unerring firmness. Henri Fluchére does not say that Eliot's is the prose of a purely intellectual writer as a subtle interplay of irony and emotion is felt throughout the pattern of the style, colouring the statements and giving to some of his pronouncements the irrefutability of profoundly experienced truth. Irony, emotional tone and rhetoric are to be noted in the following lines of Eliot taken at random from *The Idea of a Christian Society* :

The more highly industrialised the country, the more easily a materialistic philosophy will flourish in it, and the more deadly that philosophy will be. Britain has been highly industrialised longer than any other country. And the tendency of unlimited industrialism is to create bodies of men and women — of all classes — detached from tradition, alienated from religion, and susceptible to mass suggestion in other words, a mob. And a mob will be no less a mob if it is well-fed, well-clothed, well-housed, and welldisciplined.[17]

M.C. Bradbrook in her essay "Eliot's Critical Method" raises a few points concerning the critical method and style of Eliot. She notes the difference in tone and degree of force between Eliot's earlier essays and the later ones. She says that when Eliot established his own style as a poet, some informing power departed from his critical writing. If, for example, the essay "*In Memoriam*" is compared with that on Massinger, or the introduction to the volume of Kipling's verse with the essay on Dryden, it will be seen that Eliot has withdrawn from his subject : he is no longer so closely engaged. Eliot's method, Miss M.C. Bradbrook continues, is determinate in his style : a neutral style, stripped of emotional phrase and metaphor, though not without powerful resources of tone and inflexion, particularly the ironic.

It is expository rather than forensic, and works much in terms of negatives and of definition by exclusion. A series of such qualifications and restrictions :

> His conversation so nicely,
> Restricted to what, Precisely
> And If and Perhaps and But

— are to be found in Eliot. Eliot's style works by reservations and implications. In his own phrase, it has "tentacular roots". In the earlier period of his work, Eliot's criticism is criticism proper, devoid of biographical, personal, sociological digreessions, devoid also of the residue of such imperfect creative impulses as he finds in some of the criticism of Coleridge and Symons.

What Eliot says about Bradley's style in Selected Essays is true of his own. F.H. Bradley has had a great impact on Eliot's style. Eliot in the preface to his book *Knowledge and Experience in the Philosophy of F.H. Bradley* writes :

> I can present this book only as a curiosity of biographical interest, which shows, as my wife observed at once, how early my own prose style was formed on that of Bradley and how little it has changed in all these years.[18]

In Eliot's style itself one notices "a curious blend of humility and irony, and an attitude of extreme diffidence about his own work". What Eliot writes about F.H. Bradley is true of himself :

And....having in mind Bradley's polemical irony and his obvious zest in using it, his habit of discomfiting an opponent with a sudden profession of ignorance, of inability to understand, or of incapacity for abstruse thought....[19]

Eliot often informs us that he has not the mind or the capacity for abstruse thought or theorising, but we find in his essays ample theorisjng about art, poetry and criticism. We find in Eliot, as in Bradley, the habit of discomfiting an opponent with a sudden professon of ignorance, of inability to understand. M.C. Bradbrook finds Eliot's expression — "The poem, 'Gethsemane' [by Kipling] which I do not think I understand...." — tantamount to the implication — "I expect you think it is simple, but that only shows how superficial your reading is." And almost in a similar manner Eliot tells us about his inability to understand a stanza of Shelley's "To a Skylark" :

> Keen are the arrows
>   Of that silver sphere,
> Whose intense lamp narrows
>   In the white dawn clear
> Until we hardly see — we feel that it is there.

Eliot writes about this stanza :

> I should be grateful for any explanation of this stanza until now I am still ignorant of what sphere Shelley refers to or why it should have silver arrows or what the devil he means by an intense lamp narrowing in the white dawn....There may be some clues for persons more learned that I....

The tone of humility is to be found in almost all the prefaces of F. H. Bradley's books. But true humility is the quality of one who has also solid strength in himsell The man who has enough faith in himself can afford to speak poorly of himself or can dwell on his limitations with serenity and calm. Eliot has written his prefaces to his books exactly in the Bradleyan vein. Eliot says in "Shakespeare and the Stoicism of Seneca" that he has never read a more terrible exposure of human weakness — universal weakness — as in the last great speech of Othello. What Othello seems to him to be doing in making this speech is "cheering himself up" or thinking about himself. Humility, Eliot continues, is the most difficult of all virtues to achieve; nothing dies harder than the desire to think well of oneself. We may add that to talk big of oneself generally irritates the reader whereas the presentation of one's true position — of strength and of weakness — with humility and submission arouses a receptive, cooperative frame of mind in him.

William Empson records his earliest memory of Eliot in his essay "The Style of the Master". Eliot, when asked what he thought of Proust, replied, "I have not read Proust." A week after, a person asked Eliot what he thought of the translation of Proust by Scott-Moncrieff, and Eliot delivered a very weighty and long tribute to that work. William Empson and others were startlcd by so much loquacity from "the silent master". It seemed quite clear to Mr. Empson what Eliot meant when he said he had not read Proust. Eliot did not consider he had "read" a book unless he had written copious notes about it.

The *Ethical Studies*, said F.H. Bradley, "did not aim at the construction of a system of moral philosophy". The first words of the preface to his *Priticiples of Logic* are : "The following work makes no claim to supply any systematic treatment of logic." He begins the preface to *Appearatice and Reality* with "I have described the following work as an essay in metaphysics. Neither in form nor extent does it carry out the idea of a system." The phrase for each book is almost the same. We find Eliot in the prefaces to his different books writing in the same vein — In his preface to the 1928 edition of *The Sacred Wood* :

There are, it is true, faults of style which I regret; and especially I detect frequently. a stiffness and an assumption of pontifical solcmnity which may be tiresome to many readers.

In the preface of 1951 to *Selected Essays* :

I have expanded the original volume of *Selected Essays* 1917-32, by including a few essays from the now *superfluous Essays — Ancient and Modern*....But *Selectcd Essays* is already bulky enough....On reviewing the contents of the book, I find myself at times inclined to quarrel with my own judgments, and more often to criticise the way in which they were expressed.

Or in his preface to *On Poets* :

In publishing these addresses now, I have not attempted to transform them into what they might have been if originally designed for the eye instead of the ear; nor have I made alterations . . . . and also some of those preambular remarks, and incidental pleasantries, which having been intended to seduce the listeners might merely irritate the reader.

In the preface to *The Use of Poetry* :

These lectures, delivered at Harvard University....owe much to an audience only too ready to applaud merit and condone defect; but I am aware that such success as they had was largely dramatic, and that they will be still more disappointing to those who heard them....

In the preface to *The Idea of a Christian Society* :

As I have chosen to consider such a large problem, it should be obvious that the following pages can have but little importance by themselves....At most this essay can be only an original arrangement of ideas which did not belong to me before....That is a task for which I am incompetent.

In the same way, Eliot begins his preface negatively in *Notes towards the Definiition of Culture* and says that his purpose is not to outline social or political philosophy. His aim is to help define the word "culture".

And lastly in his preface to *Knowledge and Experience* :

From the autumn of 1915 until the end of 1916 I earned my living as a schoolmaster....Fortysix years after my academic philosophizing came to an end, I find myself unable to think in the terminology of this essay. Indeed I do not pretend to understand it. As philosophizing, it may appear to most modern philosophers to be quaintly antiquated. I can present this book only as a curiosity of biographical interest....

Eliot's irony is the weapon of a modest and highly sensitive man. It is usually part of the texture of Eliot's style. At one place in "The Function of Criticism", irony turns almost to ridicule :

Why have principles when one has the inner voice? If I like a thing, that is all I want; and if enough of us, shouting all together, like it, that should be all that you....ought to want.[20]

Or later in the same essay :

There is tendency, and I think it is a whiggery tendency, to decry this critical toil of the artist; to propound the thesis that the great artist is an unconscious artist, unconsciously inscribing on his banner the words Muddle Through.[21]

"Muddle Through" has been capitalised and this emphasis constitutes a pungent criticism of the belief in unconscious art. Persons who believe that a great artist is only an unconscious artist and has nothing to do with labour and critical toil, are mistaken.

Eliot is critical of the Romantic notion of poetry :

> When we talk about Poetry with capital P, we are apt
> to think only of the more intense emotion or the more
> magical phrase : nevertheless there are a great many
> casements in poetry which are not magic, and which do
> not open on the foam of perilous seas, but are perfectly
> good windows for all that.[22]

Eliot's irony does not remain always limited to tone, inflexion, single word or phrase; at times it takes the form of ruthless chastising. For example, Eliot's style in the essay on Arnold is sharp-edged and hard-hitting. It minutely analyses Arnold's expressions and finds in them a medley of flaw and falsehood. Eliot deflates Arnold's statement — "No one can deny that it is of advantage to a poet to deal with a beautiful world" — by saying that for a poet a beautiful world is not very important and the poet is supposed to see beneath both beauty and ugliness, to see the boredom and the horror and the glory.

Arnold says : "The greatness of a poet lies in his powerful and beautiful application of ideas to life." Eliot comments : "Not a happy way of putting it, as if ideas were a lotion for the inflamed skin of suffering humanity."[23] And more : "This seemed to me a striking, dangerous and subversive assertion. 'Poetry is at bottom a criticism of life.' Arnold might have read Lessing's famed *Laocoon* with a view to disentangling his own confusions."[24]

Eliot is outspoken in praise of economy, precision, and the width of emotional appeal in Dante. He cannot tolerate verbiage or looseness in exposition or expression of ideas in others or in himself.

To guide writers, George Orwell said : "If it is possible to cut out a word, cut it out." Eliot too gives this very advice to writers and poets. As a man thinks and feels, so he writes. If his thoughts are muddled, his style will be muddled. If his thoughts are clear and sharp, his writing will be clear and sharp. "A man's style," wrote Emerson, "is his mind's voice." And he added : "Wooden minds, wooden voices."[25]

The ideal task of a critic is primarily to make us possessed of facts about a work of art and not to make judgment of good and worse, But we find Arnold in his essays on Wordsworth engaged more in talking about the superiority and inferiority of a particular poet than in doing close analysis. Arnold's tone is laudatory and eulogistic and sonorous. Eliot's style when laudatory puts or lays bare before us the fact for being so. We find Arnold using words like "greatness" and "glory" without showing us the cause for such use. Arnold writes in his essay : "He (Wordsworth) is one of the very chiefest glories of English poetry; and by nothing is England so glorious as by her poetry."[26]

The language of Arnold here, strictly speaking, is not the language of criticism. To say that a particular poem or poetry is "glorious" carries sense only in a vague way.

Eliot's essay on the Metaphysical poets, though a review, is more analytical. It is suggestive and illuminating :

> On the other hand some of Donne's most successful and characteristic effects are secured by brief words and sudden contrasts. "A bracelet of bright hair about the bone." Here the most powerful effect is produced by the sudden contrast of associations of bright hair and of bone.[27]

F.R. Leavis at his best is analytical and critical but too seriously engaged in his work to take care to delight the reader. "Seriousness" is the key word for the temperament shown in his critical essays. Dr. Leavis makes an important point while introducing his book *Revaluation* "But no treatment of poetry is worth much that does not keep very close to the concrete : there lies the problem of the method."[28] But one finds in his criticism veiled prejudices and prepossessions. Eliot in his essay "To Criticise the Critic" says about Leavis : "And another critic of importance, Dr. F.R. Leavis, who may be called the critic as Moralist."[29]

REFERENCES

1. Quoted by H. Coombes, *Literature and Criticism*, Pelican Book, p. 8.
2. Middleton Murry, *The Problem of Style*, Oxford Paperback, No. II, pp. 6-7.
3. *To Criticize the Critic*, p. 14.
4. *Ibid.*, p. 16.

5. *The Sacred Wood.*
6. *To Criticise the Critic.*
7. *Ibid.*
8. *The Criterion.*
9. *Ibid.*
10. *A Short Guide to English Style,* Oxford University Press, 1961, p. 181.
11. *The Sacred Wood,* p. 147.
12. *Ibid.*
13. *To Criticize the Critic,* p. 32.
14. *The Sacred Wood,* p. 79.
15. *Ibid.,* p. 49.
16. *Ibid.,* p. 51.
17. *The Idea of a Christian Society,* 4th impression, p. 21.
18. *Knowledge and Experience,* p. 10.
19. *Selected Essays,* p. 445.
20. *Ibid,* p. 30.
21. *Ibid.*
22. *On Poetry and Poets,* p. 49.
23. *The Use of Poetry,* p. 112.
24. *Ibid.,* p. 113.
25. Quoted by Alan Warner, *A Short Guide to English Style,* Oxford University Press, 1961.
26. Arnold, *Essays in Criticism,* 2nd Series, p. 96.
27. *Selected Essays,* p. 283.
28. *Revaluation,* Chatto & Windus, 1953, p. 2.
29. *To Criticize the Critic,* p. 13.

8

Conclusions

T.S. Eliot belongs to the great tradition of English criticism, headed by Dryden, Dr. Johnson, Coleridge and Matthew Arnold. From time to time, every hundred years or so, it is desirable that some critic should appear to "review the past of our literature and set the poets and the poems in a new order." This task, says Eliot, is not of revolution but of readjustment. And Eliot has successfully performed this task for his age.

In an interview with Ranjee Shahani, Eliot said : "What I seem to have accomplished in criticism is to have altered emphases in criticism and revived interest in certain writers."[1]

Eliot's formulations regarding poetry are of paramount importance. Unlike Edgar Allan Poe, Eliot says that a good long poem is a reality, and the poet should not be striving all the time for poetic intensity. It is not essential that a poet must always pour fourth poetry ecstatic, exquisite and magical; he should also be capable of writing "verse". For a long impersonal poem, it is essential that the poetic and the prosaic, or the "poetry" and the "verse" should coexist.

Eliot says that "rhetorical" should not be always used as a term of abuse. He distinguishes[2] between the rhetoric of manner and the rhetoric of substance. Good rhetoric issues from the substance or from what the author has to express.

Eliot has enriched English criticism by his novel and seminal ideas. According to Mathiessen the critical illustrations of Eliot are like segments from which we can easily draw circles.

Eliot combines, in criticism, to a remarkable degree, sensitiveness, erudition, a sense of fact, a sense of history, and genealishing power. Ezra Pound wrote an essay on Eliot with the title "Mr. Eliot's Solid Merit"[3] and prescribed for the reader a solid study of Eliot. William Empson remarked that Eliot has a very "penetrating influence perhaps not unlike an east wind."[4] And this is true not only of Eliot's poetry but also his criticism. I.A. Richards says that "in one degree or another we are all products of his work."[5]

Dr. Leavis's *Revaluation* owes very much, in its handling of the ideas of tradition and of "the line of Wit", to the early essays of Elliot. A great deal of current criticism of poetry reads like foot notes to Eliot's critical ideas. Even when the critical terms of Eliot do not have universal validity, they are a permanent source of stimulus to our critical sensibility.

While introducing Fluchére's book on Shakespeare, Eliot points out the requisites of an ideal Shakespeare critic. He himself as critic seems to fulfil those requisites. Eliot has done more than anyone to promote "the shift of sensibility" away from the Georgians. The unity of Eliot's critical thought is not the unity attained by a man who never changes his mind, but the unity that obtains in the total wok of a man who has never ceased to grow and to mature. Professor Grand T. Webster says[6] that Eliot's criticism is valuable like Dr. Johanson's not beacuse of the subject and not beacuse what he says is right or wrong but because we can experience in his writings "a first class mind in action", and can learn one possible response to literature and life. F.R. Leavis finds "the fine intelligence at least in Eliot's earlier and larger collection"[7]

REFERENCES

1. "T.S. Eliot Answers Questions", by Ranjee Shahani (included in *T.S. Eliot : Homage from India*, ed. by P. Lal (Writers Workshop, 1965), p. 131.

2. *The Sacred Wood*, p.79.

3. *T.S. Eliot*, ed. by Hugh Kenner, p. 149.

4. *Ibid.*, p. 152.

5. *Eliot and his Work*, ed. by Allen Tate, 196. p. 1.

6. "Eliot as Critic", *Criticism*, Fall, 1966, Vol. VIII. No, 4, p. 339.

7. F.R. Leavis, "Eliot's Stature as Critic", *Commentary*, XXVI, Nov. 1958, p. 399.

Appendix

Critic as Avoider of Formulae

T.S. Eliot says : "The true critic is a scrupulous avoider of formulae; he refrains from statements which pretend to be literally true; he finds facts nowhere and approximation always. His truths are truths of experience rather than calculation."[1]

Though Eliot's doctoral dissertation is on the philosophy of F.H. Bradley it needs to be interpreted by us in terms of critical aesthetics. Eliot's admiration for F.H. Bradley has been known ever since he quoted that philosopher in the notes to *The Waste Land*. Professor Hugh Kenner in *The Invisible* Poet says that there is a considerable influence exerted by F.H. Bradley on T.S. Eliot the poet and critic. Eliot writes : "I find myself now, forty-five years after my philosophizing came to an end, unable to think in the terminology of the essay. Indeed, I do not pretend to understand it."[2]

And in fact *Knowledge and Experience* is a philosophical study by Eliot not easily grasped by a student of literature. But if comprehended it opens before us novel literary critical horizons and possibilities.

This book of Eliot has not been explored and discussed from this angle yet, so I have deliberately chosen the title of the paper from *Knowledge and Experience*.

It is true to say that a true critic is a scrupulous avoider of formulae. The mind of a good, sensitive critic is a free, unprejudiced mind. The aim of criticism is to find the object as it really is. This ideal cannot be achieved by a critic unless he is free from preconceived ideas and set formulae. An aesthetic law or formula, however good and exhaustive, may not help us in the assessment of the beauty and excellence of a work of art of a new kind. What Lord David Cecil writes in his essay. "The Fine Art of Reading" echoes Eliot's statement about a critic :

> All this should put us on our guard against starting to read any book with preconceived ideas of what it ought or ought not to be like. For this reason rigid systems of aesthetic law....rules of design and composition and vocabulary and so on....are to be viewed with suspicion....The socalled laws of art are only tentative generalizations drawn from the observation of particular works and cannot completely apply to an original work.[3]

A true critic is an avoider of formulae in the sense that he goes to the work of art straight and makes a sensitive reading and close analysis of it. A committed critic is much less a critic. His vision and judgement will be partial, lopsided and fragmentary. A committed or a dogmatic critic is constantly guided by his pre-nourished dogmas. He is the most erratic in applying his favourite dogma as a test for the success or failure of a particular work of art. Eliot writes :

> The dogmatic critic who lays down a rule, who affirms a value, has left his labour incomplete. Such statements may often be justifiable as a saving of time; but in matters of great importance the critic must not coerce, and he must not make judgements of worse and better. He must simply elucidate; the reader will form the correct judgement for himself.

The function of criticism is the elucidation of the work of art and the correction of taste, and the task of a critic is to help us understand and enjoy a work of art. The usual known formula is that in a drama there must be the three unities. But a dramatist can achieve success even without this, if he maintains emotional unity. Similarly a writer cannot be dubbed "bad" simply because he does not use colloquial or spoken speech. Lord David Cecil writes :

> ....equally foolish is the modern reviewer who rebukes a poet for not employing what he hideously calls a "contemporary vocabulary". The only test of a book's merit is the impression it makes on the reader. If the

reader is pleased, it does not matter how many socalled rules of art the author has broken.[4]

The critic's truths, says Eliot, are truths of experience rather than calculation. Any formula or generalization about art or poetry is only one man's account. That a critic should avoid formula is a pointer towards the fact that he should assess a work of art having apprehended it, or lived into it immediately or directly. Edumumd Gosset says; "Poetry is not a formula which a thousand flappers and hobbledehoys ought to be able to master in a week...."

And almost in the same vein we can say that criticism is not a ready made maxim to be remembered and to be used and applied by any self-appointed satrap at his sweet will. Eliot writes : "English criticism is inclined to argue or persuade (or to formulate) rather than to state; and, instead of forcing the subject to expose himself...it is difficult, it is perhaps the supreme difficulty of criticism to make the facts generalize themselves."[5]

A critic should make the facts generalize themselves and should not apply generalization itself to a particular work of art. What Dr. F.R. Leavis writes is very much pertinent to the present issue : "But no treatment of poetry is worth much that does not keep very close to the concrete...The rule of a critic is or should (I think) be, to work as much as possible in terms of particular analysis...of poems or passages, and to say nothing that cannot be related immediately to judgement about producible texts."[6]

Dr. Wellek, discussing Dr. Leavis' book (Revaluation), says : "Now allow me to sketch your (Dr. Leavis') idea of poetry, your 'norm' with which you measure every poet..."[7]

But this suggests a false idea of the procedure of a good critic. Words in poetry invite us not "to think about" and judge but to "feel into" or "become", to realise the complex experience that is given in the words. They demand a full-bodied response that is incompatible with the judicial, one-eye-on-the — standard approach suggested by Dr. Wellek's phrase : "Your 'norm' with which you measure every poet."

Statements made by a literary critic are not literal truths since a work of art, even when fully understandable and enjoyable, has after all an aura of idefinable experience and evanescent shoots of feeling and tentacular roots of complexity. A piece of criticism however good and objective cannot be the last word. The process of criticism is the eradication of one error by another. In the field of criticism there is nothing like a truce and not a clean victory or defeat. Then what is the use of literary criticism? This is very pertinent question worth asking again and again even if we find no satisfactory answer. Criticism may be what F.H. Bradley said of metaphysics — "the finding of bad reasons for what we believe upon instinct but finding this reason is no less as instinct." A critic searches facts concerning a work of art in order to put it before us in such a way that we may not be prejudiced against it. But in fact he does not find verifiable facts but approximations towards facts. A single poem may be interpreted differently by different sensitive readers. And all the interpretations may be valid or significant.

Eliot writes : "I remember a phrase of Dickens ('There are no private truths'). I do not recall the context and am not concerned with the meaning which the phrase had there; but I should reverse the decision, and say : all significant truths are private truths; as they become public, they cease to become truth, they become...at best, part of the public character, or at worst, words."[8]

The critic's truths are truths of experience rather than of calculation as the critic deals with art and the artist. Life, says Virginia Woolf, is not a series of gig lamps symmetrically arranged. It is luminous halo, a semi-transparent envelope surrounding our consciousness from the beginning to the end. The artist apprehends this very mystery of human life. The critic also has an inkling of this mystery while studying the work of art, and bases his judgement upon impressions which subsist upon the text. Fliot in his essay "The Perfect Critic" says that not only all knowledge, but all feeling is in perception. Some critic once observed that "poetry is the most highly organised form of intellectual activity". Such a statement may be taken as a specimen of the abstract style in criticism. The inventor of poetry as "the most highly organised form of intellectual activity" was not engaged in perceiving when he composed this definition.

A good critic is always empirical as Eliot is. He does not feel shy in changing, reversing, negating or criticizing his own previous formulation or opinion in the light of a new experience. His one critical opinion of a time is not to be taken as a permanent calculating machine to test the fitness, richness, vitality or significance of the new work of art.

A piece of criticism, however dispassionate and impartial or calculated, cannot be pure science.

REFERENCES

1. *Knowledge and Experience*, p. 164.
2. *Ibid.*, p. 10.
3. *English Critical Essays*, 20th Century, 2nd series, p. 186.
4. *Ibid.*
5. *Selected Essays* (Faber), p. 205.
6. *Revaluation* (Pelican), p. 10.
7. *The Common Pursuit* (1952), p. 10.
8. *Knowledge and Experience*, p. 165.

SELECT BIBLIOGRAPHY

Critical Works by Eliot

Books and Pamphlets

Ezra Pound, His Metric and Poetry; New York : Knopf, 1917.

The Sacred Wood : Essays on Poetry and Criticism; London : Methuen & Co., Ltd. 1920.

For Lancelot Andrews : Essays on Style and Order; London : Faber & Gwyer, 1928.

John Dryden : The Poet, the Dramatist, the Critic; New York : Terence & Elsa Holiday, 1932.

Selected Essays : 1917-32. New York : Harcourt, Brace & Co., 1932 (New Edition, 1950).

The Use of Poetry and the Use of Criticism : Studies In Relation of Criticism to Poetry in England, London, Faber & Faber, 1933.

After Strange Gods : A Primer of Modern Heresy; London : Faber & Faber, 1934.

Elizabethan Essays, London : Faber & Faber, 1934.

Essays Ancient and Modern; London : Faber & Faber, 1936.

The idea of a Christian Society; London : Faber & Faber, 1939.

The Music of Poetry, Glasgow : Jackson, Son & Co., 1942.

From Poe to Valéry, New York : Harcourt, Brace & Co., 1948.

Notes towards the Definition of Culture; London : Faber & Faber, 1948.

Essays by T. S. Eliot, edited by Kazumi Yano; Tokyo Henkyusha, 1951.

American Literature and American Language : An Address Delivery at Washington University on June 9, 1953. With an appendix of the Eliot family in St. Louis, perpared by the Department of English; Washington University Studies, n. s. : Language and Literature No. 23; St. Louis : Washington University, Committee on Publications, 1953.

Selected Prose : Edited by John Hayward; London : Penguin Books in association with Faber & Faber, 1953.

Religious Drama : Mediaeval and Modern; New York House of Books Ltd., 1954.

The Literature of Politics : A Lecture Delivered at a C.P.C. Literary Luncheon; London : Conservative Political Centre, 1955.

Essays on Elizabethan Drama; New York : Harcourt, Brace & Co., 1956.

On Poetry and Poets; New York : Farrar, Straus & Cudahy, 1957.

George Herbert, London : Published by Longmans, Green & Co. for The British Council and the National Book League, 1962.

Knowledge and Experience in the Philosophy of F.H. Bradley; London : Faber, 1964.

To Criticize the Critic and Other Writings; New York : Farrar, Straus & Giroux, 1965.

Contributions to Books

"A Brief Introduction to the Method of Paul Valéry". *Le Serpent* par Paul Valéry. Translated by Mark Wardle; London, Cobden-Sanderson 1924, pp. 7-15. "Introduction", *Savonarola,* by Charlotte Eliot; London Cobden-Sanderson, 1926; pp. vii-xii.

"Introduction", *Ezra Pound : Selected Poems*, edited by T.S. Eliot; London : Faber & Gwyer, 1928. pp. vii-xxv.

"Introduction", *The Wheel of Fire*, by G. Wilson Knight; London : Oxford University Press, 1930, pp. xi-xix.

"Donne in Our Time", *A Garland for John Donne* : 1631-1931; edited by Theodore Spencer; Cambridge, Massr. : Harvard University Press, 1931; pp. 1-19.

"Preface", *Transit of Venu* : Poems by Harry Crosby; Black Sun Press, 1931; pp. i-ix.

"Preface", *Bubu of Montparnasse*, by Charles-Louis Philippe; translated by Laurence Vail; Paris : Crosby Continental Editions, 1932, pp. vii-xiv.

"A Critical Note", *The Collected Poems of Harold Monro*, edited by Alida Monro; London : Cobden-Sanderson, 1933. pp. xiii-xvi.

"Johnson's *London and the Vanity of Human Wishes*", *English Critical Essays : Twentieth Century*; edited by Phyllis M. Jones; London : Oxford University Press, 1923; pp. 301-10. First appeared as "Introductory Essay" to *London : A Poem and The Vanity of Human Wishes by* Samuel Johnson; London : Etchells & Macdonald, 1930.

Shakespearean Criticism : From Dryden to Coleridge," *A Companion to Shakespeare Studies*; edited by Harley Granville-Barker and G.B. Harrison, Cambridge University Press, 1934; pp. 287-99.

"Introduction" Selected Poems by Marianne Moore; New York : Macmillan Co., 1935; pp. vii-xvi.

"A Note on the Verse of Milton", *Essays and Studies by Members of the English Association*, Vol. XXI, edited by Herbert Read; Oxford : Clarendon Press, 1936; pp. 32-40.

"Poetry and Propaganda", *Literary Opinion in America*, edited by M.D. Zabel; New York : Harper & Brothers, 1937; pp. 25-28. First appeared in Bookman LXX, No. 6 (February, 1930), 595-602.

"Revelation", *Revelation* by Gustaf Aulen and others; edited by John Baille and Hugh Martin; London : Faber & Faber, 1937; pp. 1-39.

"A Note on Two Odes of Cowley", *Seventeenth Century Studies Presented to Sir Herbert Grierson*; Oxford Clarendon Press, 1938; pp. 235-42.

"Preface", *Anabasis : A Poem*, by St. J. Perse; New York : Harcourt Brace & Co., 1938 : pp. 7-11. First English Edition by Faber & Faber in 1930.

"A Note on War Poetry", *London Calling*, edited by Storm Jameson; New York : Harper & Brothers, 1942; pp. 237-38.

"Civilization : The Nature of Cultural Relations", *Friendship, Progress, Civilization* : Speeches to the Anglo-Swedish Society by Lord Sempill, Harold Nicolson, and T.S. Eliot; London : Anglo-Swedish Society, 1943; pp.15-20.

"Introduction", *Shakespeare and the Popular Dramatic Tradition*, by S.L. Bethell; Westminster P.S. King & Staples Ltd., 1943; pp. 7-9.

"Lecon de Valéry", *Paul Valéry*, Marseille Cahiers du Sud, 1946; pp. 74-81.

"Preface", *The Dark Side of the Moon*; New York, Charles Scribner's Sons, 1947, pp. vii-x.

"Introduction", *All Hallow's Eve*, by Charles Williams; New York : Pellegrini & Cudahy, 1948; pp. ix-xviii.

"*Ulysses*, Order, and Myth", *James Joyce : Two Decades of Criticism*, edited by Seon Givens, New York : Vanguard Press, Inc., pp. 198-202.

"Preface", *English Poetry and its contribution to the Knowledge of a Creative Principle*, by Leone Vivante; London : Faber & Faber, 1950; pp. vii-xi.

"Foreword", *Cantemporary French Poetry*, by Joseph Chiari, New York : Philosophical Library, 1952; pp. vii-xi.

"Foreword", *Shakespeare*, by Henri Fluchére; London; Longmans, Green & Co., 1953 ; pp. vi-vii.

"Introduction", *Literary Essays* by Ezra Pound, edited by T.S. Eliot : London : Faber & Faber, 1954; pp. ix-xv.

"Foreword", *Symbolism from Poe to Mallaré, the Growth of a Myth*, by Joseph Chiari; London : Rockliff, 1956: pp. V-Viii.

"Introduction", *The Art of Poetry* (The Collected Works of Paul Valéry, edited by J. Matthews, Vol. VII.) : New York Pantheon Books, 1958. Available in paperback.

Contributions to Periodicals

"The Letters of J.B. Yeats", *Egoist*, IV, No. 6 (July, 1917), 89-90.

"Reflections on Contemporary Poetry, I'' *Egoist*, IV, No. 8 (September 1917), 118-19.

"Reflections on Contemporary Poetry, 11" *Egoist*, IV, No. 9 (October 1917), 133-34.

"Reflections on Contemporary Poetry, III" *Egoist*, IV, No. 10 (November 1917), 151.

"Disjecta Membra", *Egoist*, V, No. 4 (April 1918), 55.

"Observations", *Egoist*, V, No. 5 (May 1918), 69-70.

"Contemporanca", *Egoist*, V, No. 6 (June 1918), 84-85.

"Studies in Contemporary Criticism, 11", *Egoist*, V, No. 10. (November 1918), 131-33.

"Beyle and Balzac", *Athenaeum*, No. 4648 (May 1919); pp. 392-93.

"Criticism in England", *Athenaeum*, No. 4650 (June 1919), pp, 456-57.

"The Education of Taste", *Athenaeum*, No. 4652 (June 1919), pp. 520-21.

"A Foreign Mind", *Athenaeum*, No. 4653 (July 1919), pp, 552-53.

"Reflections on Contemporary Poetry IV, 9, *Egoist*, VI, No. 3 (July 1919), 39-40.

"Was There a Scottish Literature?" *Athenaeum*, No. 4657 (August 1919), pp. 680-81.

"Humanist, Artist and Scientist", *Athenaeum*, No. 4667 (October 1919), pp. 1014-15.

"War-Paint and Feathers" *Athenaeum*, No. 4668 (October 1919), p. 1036.

"A Brief Treatise on the Criticism of Poetry", *Chapbook*, 11, No. 9 (March 1920), 1-10.

"Modern Tendencies in Poetry", *Shamáa*, I, No. I (April 1920), 9-18.

"Artists and Men of Genius", *Athenaeum*, No. 4704, (June 25, 1920), p. 4S2.

"Prose and Verse", *Chapbook*, XXII (April 1921), 3-10. "London Letter", *Dial*, LXXT, No. 2 (August 1921), 213-17.

"London Letter", *Dial*, LXXII, No. 5 (April 1922), 510-13.

"Notes on Current Letters : The Romantic Englishman, The Comic Spirit, and The Function of Criticism The Lesson of Baudelaire", *Tyro*, I (1922), 4.

"Dramatis Personae", *Criterion*, I, No 3 (April, 1923), 303-6.

"John Donne", *Nation & Athenaeum*, XXXIII, No. 10 (June 1923), 331-32.

"The Function of a Llterary Review", *Criterion*, 1, No. 4, (July 1923), 421.

"Andrew Marvell", *Nation & Athenaeum*, XXXIII, No. 26 (September 1923), 809.

"*Ulysses*, Order, and Myth", *Dial*, LXXV, 5 (November 1923), 480-83.

"Marianne Moore", *Dial*, LXXV, No. 6 (December 1923), 594-97.

"A Letter to the Editor : F.M. Ford", *Transatlantic Review*, 1, No. I (January 1924), 95-96.

"A Commentary", *Criterion*, II, No. 7 (April 1924), 231-35.

"The Ballet", *Criterion*, 111, No. I I (April 1925), 441-43.

"Shakespeare and Montaigne", *Times Literary Supplement*, 1249 (December 24, 1925), p, 895.

"The Idea of a Literary Review", *Criterion*, IV, No. 1 (January 1926) 1-6.

"Creative Criticism", *Times Literary* (August 12 1926), p. 535.

"Chaucer's Troilus", *Times Literary* (August 19 1926), p. 547.

"Mr. Read and Mr. Fernandez", *Criterion* IV, No. 4 (October 1926), 751-57.

"Whitman and Tennyson", Nation and *Athenaeum* XI, No. II (December 1926), 426.

"A Note on Poetry and Belief", *Enemy*, I (January 1927), 15-17.

'The Problems of the Shakespeare Sonnets", *Nation & Athenaeum*, XL, No. 19 (February 1927), 664, 666.

"Literature, Science, and Dogma" *Dial*, LXXXII, No. 3 (March 1927), 239-43.

"A Study of Marlowe", *Times Literary Supplement*, No. 1309 (March 1927), p. 140.

"Poet and Saint. . ." *Dial*, LXXXII, No. 5 (May 1927), 424-31.

"A Commentary", *Criterion*, V, No. 3 (June 1927), 283-86.

"A Commentary", *Criterion*, VI, No. 2 (1927) 97-100.

'The Silurist", *Dial*, LXXXIIII, No. 3 (September 1927), 259-63.

"Isolated Superiority", *Dial*, 1XXXIV, No. 1 (1928), 4.7.

"Mr. Lucas's Webster", *Criterion*, VII, No. 4 (June 1928), 155-58.

"Experiment in Criticism", *Bookman*, LXX, No. 3 (November 1929), 225-33.

"Poetry and Propaganda", *Bookman*, LXX, No. 6 (February 1930), 595-602. Reprinted in *Literary Opinion in America*, edited by M. D. Zael; New York : Harper & Brothers, 1937, pp 25-38.

"Thinking in Verse : A Survey of Early 17th Century Poetry", *Listener*, III, No. 61 (March 1930), 441-43.

"Rhyme and Reason : The Poetry of John Donne", *Listener*, 111, No. 62 (March 1930), 502-3.

"Mystic and Politician as Poet : Vaughan, Traherne, Marvell, Milton", *Listener*, III, No. 64 (April 1930), 590-91.

"A Commentary", *Criterion*, X, No. 40 (April 1931), 481-90.

"A Review of *Son of Woman : The Story of D.H. Lawrence*", *Criterion* X, No. 41 (July 1931), 768-74.

"A Commentary", *Criterion*, XI, No. 42 (October 1931), 65-72.

"A Commentary", *Criterion*, XI, No. 45 (July 1932), 676-83.

"A Commentary", *Criterion*, XII, No. 46 (October 1932), 73-79.

"A Commentary", *Criterion*, XII, No. 47 (January 1933), 244-49.

"A Commentary", *Criterion*, XII, No. 49 (July 1933), 642-47.

"A Commentary", *Criterion*, XIII, No. 53 (July 1934), 624-30.

"The Problem of Education", *Harvard Advocate*, CXXI, No. I (Freshman, November 1934), 11-12.

"A Commentary", *Criterion*, XIV, No. 54 (October 1934), 86-90.

"A Commentary", *Criterion*, XIV, No. 57 (July 1935), 610-13.

"Literature and the Modern World", *American Prefaces*, 1, No. 2 (November 1935), 19-22.

"Mr. Murry's Shakespeare", *Criterion*, XV, No-61 (July 1936), 708-10.

"A Commentary" *Criterion*, XVII, No. 66 (October 1937), 81-86.

"A Commentary : That Poetry is Made with Words", *New English Weekly*, XV, No. 2 (April 1939), 27-28.

"That Poetry is Made with Words": a letter to the editor, *New English Weekly*, XV, No. 4 (May 1939), 66.

"The Duchess of Malfi", *Listener*, XXVI, No. 675 (December 1941), 825-26.

"A Dream within a Dream : T.S. Eliot on Edgar Allan Poe", *Listener*, XXIX, No. 737 (February 1943), 243-44.

"The Approach to James Joyce", *Listener*, XXX, No. 770 (October 1943), 446-47.

"Ezra Pound", *Poetry*, LXVIII, No. 6 (September 1946), 926-38.

"A Talk on Dante", *Kenyon Review*, XIV, No. I (Winter, 1952), 178-88. First appeared as "Talk on Dante", *Italian News*, No. 2 (July 1950), 13-18.

"On Teaching the Appreciation of Poetry", *Teachers College Record*, LXII, No. 3 (December 1986), 215-21.

Selected Periodical Articles

Adams, J.D. : Speaking of Books *New York Times Books Review,* Dec. 16, 1956, LXI, 3.

Adams, R.M. : Donne and Eliot : Metaphysicals *Kenyon Review* Spring 1954, XVI, pp. 278-91.

Allen, Walter : The Time and Place of T.S. Eliot, *New York Times Book Review,* April 9, p. 1, 40,1961.

Alvarez, A, : Eliot and Yeats : Orthodoxy and Tradition, *Twentieth Century* Aug.& Sept. 1957, CLXII, 149-63.

Anon : Eliot and an Age of Fiction, *New Statesman,* Jan. 8, p. 47, 1965.

Anon : Great Man Gone, *Times Literary Supplement,* 1965 Jan. 7, p. 9.

Austin, Allen : T.S. Eliot's Theory of Dissociation, *College English,* 1962, XXIII, 309-12.

Auden, W.H. : T.S. Eliot —O.M.— A Tribute, *Listener,* Jan. 7, 1965, V. 3, p. 5.

Blackmur, R.P. : Mr. Eliot and the Notion of Culture, *Partisan Review,* 1944, Summer, XI, 302-12, 1944.

Blissett, William F. : T.S. Eliot, *Canadian Forum* July, xxviii, 86-73, 1948.

Blissett, William F. : Pater and Eliot, *University of Toronto Quarterly,* April 1953, 261-8.

Breit, Harvey : An Interview with Eliot, *New York, Times Book Review,*Nov. 21, p. 3, 1948.

Brown (E.K.) : Mr. Eliot and Some Enemies, *University of Toronto Quarterly,* VIII, 69-84, 1938.

Blackmur, R.P. : In the hope of straightening things out, *Kenyon Review Spring,* 1951,V, 12, p. 303-14.

Blanshard, B. : Eliot in Memory, *Yale Review* June 1965, LIV, 635-40.

Bollier, E. P. : Eliot and F.H. Bradley, *Tulane Studies in English,* 1963, XII, 87-111.

Bollier, E.P. : Eliot and The Sacred Wood, *The Colorado Quarterly,* VIII, 308-17, 1960.

Bordwell, H. : Remembering Eliot, *Chicago Review Summer-Autumn,* 1984, XVII, 33-6.

Braybrooke, N. : Thomas Stearns Eliot, *Contemporary Review* Sept. 1958, CXCIV, 123-6.

Child, R. C. : The Early Critical Work of Eliot, *College Engtish,* Feb. 1951. XII, 269-75.

Ciardi, J. : T.S. Eliot, 1888-1965, *Saturday Review,* Jan. 23, 1965, p. 35-6.

Chase, Richard : Eliot in Concord *Asc., Autumn,* XVI, 438-43, 1947.

Collin, W.E. : Eliot the Critic, *Saturday Review,* XXXIX, 419-24, 1931.

Coxe, Louis O. : Winters on Eliot, *Kenyon Review,* Autumn, 14, 498-500, 1941.

Davie, D. : Eliot : the End of an Era, *20th Century,* April 1956, CLIX 350-62.

De Laura, D.S. : Pater and Eliot, *Modern Language Quarterly,* Sept. 1965, XXVI, 426-31

Ellmann, Richard : Yeats and Eliot, *Encounter,* 1965, July, XXV, 53-5.

Frank, Waldo : Universe of Eliot, *Adelphi* Feb. V, 321-5, 1933.

Gardner, Helen : The "Agéd Eagle" spreads his wings, *Sunday Times* Sept. 21, 1958, p. 8.

Glicksberg, Charles 1. : Eliot as Critic, *Arizona Quarterly,* iv, 225-26.

Grigson, Geoffrey : Leavis against Eliot, *Encounter* April 1959, xii, 68-9.

Gross, John : Eliot, from Ritual to Realism, *Encounter,* March 1965, XXIV, 48-50.

Hewes, Henry : Eliot on Eliot, *Saturday Review,* Sept. 13, 1958, p. 32.

Holder, Alan : Eliot on Henry James, *PMLA,* Sept. 1964, LXXIX, 490-7.

Howarth, Herbert : Eliot and Milton, *University of Toronto Quarterly,* 1961, XXX, 150-62.

Hyman, Stanley Edgar : Eliot : 1888-1965, *The New Leader,* Feb. 1, 1965, p. 21-2.

Jarrell, R. : The T.S. Eliot Myth, *New York Times Book Review,* Nov. 18, 1951, p. 36.

Knieger, Bernard : The Dramatic Achievement of Eliot, *Modern Drama*, 1961, 111 387-92.

Kornbluth, Martin L. : A 20th Century "Everyman", *College English*, 1960, XXI, 26-9.

Leavis, F.R. : Eliot and Milton, *Studies in Romanticism*, March 1949, LVII, 1-30.

Levy, William Turner : A Memoir of Eliot, *N.Y. Times Book Review*, Jan. 31, 1965, p. 34-5.

Marks, Emerson R. : Eliot and the Ghost of S.T.C., *Sewanee Review Spring*, 1964, LXXTI, 262-80.

Maxwell, J.C. : Eliot and Husserl, *Notes and Queries* (N.S.) Feb. 1964, XI, 74.

McElderry, B.R. : Santayana & Eliot's objective correlative, *Boston University Studies*, Autumn, 1957 III, 179-81.

Paul, Leslie : A Conversation with Eliot, *Kenyon Review*, XXVII, 1965, 11-21.

Pound, Ezra : Eliot and Pound, *Times Literary Supplement*, July 26, 1957, 457.

Price, Martin : The Eliot Myth : *Yale Review*, XLI, 458-61.

Redman, Ben Ray : The Eliot Myth, *Saturday Review*, Feb. 2, 1952, p. 19.

Russel, Francis : Some non-encounters with Eliot, *Horizon Autumn*, 1965, VII, 37-41.

Schwartz, Delmore : The Literary Dictatorship of Eliot, *Partisan Review*, 1949.

Seymour-Smith, Martin : The Revolutionaries, *Spectator*, March 12, 1965, p. 331.

Sharpiro, Karl : Eliot : The Death of Literary Judgment, *Saturday Review*, Feb. 27, 1960 p. 12-17, 34-6.

Speaight, Robert : Remembering Eliot, *Encounter*, April 1965, XXIV, 3-14.

Speaight, Robert : Eliot O.M. : A Birthday Tribute, *Listener*, Sept. 25, 1958, LX, 455-57.

Steadman, John M. : Eliot and Husserl, *Notes and Queries*, June 1958, CCIII, 261-2.

Stevenson, David L. : An objective correlative for Hamlet, *Journal of Aesthetics & Art Criticism,* Sept. 1964.

Wain, John : Eliot *Encounter,* March 1965, XXIV, 51-3.

Vivas, Eliseo : Objective Correlative of T.S. Eliot, *American Bookman,* 1944, Winter, 1, 7, 10.

Williamson, Hugh Ross : Eliot and his Conception of Poetry, *Bookman* March, lxxxix, 347-50, 1931.

Winters, Yvor : Eliot : The Illusion of Reaction, *Kenyon Review,* Winter, III, 1941, Spring, 111, 1941.

Wassertom, William : Eliot and "The Dial", *Sewanee Review* Winter, 1962, LXX, 81-92.

Waston, George : The Triumph of Eliot, *Critical Quartorly,* Winter, 1965, VII, 328-37.

Wellel, René : The Criticism of Eliot, *Studies in Romanticism,* Summer, 1956, LXIV, 398-43.

Williams., Raymond : Second Thoughts : Eliot on Culture, *Essays in Criticism,* July 1956, IV, 302-18.

Williamson, George : Eliot, 1888-1965, *Modern Age* Fall, 1965, IX, 399-407.

Wilson Richard : The Continuity of Eliot, *Kanof,* 1965, No. 1, p. 24-32.

Some Biographical and Critical Studies

(Place of publication London, unless stated otherwise)

The Lamp and the Lute, by B. Dobrée ; Oxford (1929), Contains a critical essay on Eliot's early work.

Axel's Castle, by E. Wilson; New York (1931) Contains the first important critical estimate of Eliot's work.

The Critical Ideas of T.S. Eliot, by A Oras; Tartu Dorpat (1932).

Men Without Art, by Wyndham Lewis (1934). Contains a long critique.

The Achievement of T.S. Eliot, by F.O. Matthiessen (1935).

T.S. Eliot : A Study of his Writings by Various Hands, ed. B. Rajan (1947).

T.S. Eliot : A Selected Critique, ed. L. Unger; New York (1948).

T.S. Eliot : A Symposium, compiled by R. March and Tambimuttu.

Six Essays on the Development of T.S. Eliot, by F. Wilson (1948).

The Art of T.S. Eliot, by Helen Gardner (1949).

T.S. Eliot : The Design of his Poetry, by E. Drew; New York (1949).

Poetry and Belief in the Works of T.S. Eliot, by K. Smidt; Oslo (1949).

A Reader's Guide to T.S. Eliot, by G. Williamson; New York (1953).

The Emperor's Clothes, by K. Nott (1953), Contains a spirited attack on Eliot's orthodoxy.

T.S. Eliot's Poetry and Plays, by G. Smith, Jr; Chicago (1956).

The Shaping Spirit, by A. Alvarez (1958).

T.S. Eliot : A Symposium, ed. N. Braybrooke (1958).

Poetry and Morality : Studies on the Criticism of M. Arnold, T.S. Eliot and F.R. Leavis, by V. Buckley (1959).

The invisible Poet : T.S. Eliot, by H. Kenner (1960).

The Plays of T.S. Eliot, by D.E. Jones (1960).

T.S. Eliot, by L. Unger; Minneapolis, Minnesota (1961).

Experience Into Words, by D.W. Harding (1963).

English Dramatic Form, by M.C. Bradbook (1965), Contains a chapter on Eliot's dramas.

The Making of The Cocktail Party, by E. Martin Browne, The Judith E. Wilson Lecture, Cambridge, 1966.

T.S. Eliot and the English Poetic Tradition, by Helen L. Gardner. The Byron Lecture, Nothingham, (1966).

T.S. Eliot : The Dialectical Structure of his Theory of Poetry, by Fei-Pai-Lu, University of Chicago (1966).

T.S. Eliot : The Man and his Work, ed. Allen Tate (1967).